modern designs *for*
CLASSIC QUILTS

KELLY BISCOPINK AND ANDREA JOHNSON

12 TRADITIONALLY INSPIRED PATTERNS MADE NEW

kp

KRAUSE PUBLICATIONS
CINCINNATI, OHIO

Contents

Introduction

We both had been quilting and sewing on our own for years, and we found a crazy amount of joy in the act of creating and experimenting all on our own. It wasn't until quilt blogs started popping up a few years ago—all bold and bright with the fabrics we loved and the patterns we wanted to try—that we thought, maybe there are more like us! And sure enough, there were. Quilters and sewists started to come out of the proverbial woodwork, filling our noggins with quilt inspiration. We soaked up these blogs and online forums with zeal, all along longing for some proof that these cyberquilters actually existed.

The first meeting of our branch of The Modern Quilt Guild was absolutely like going on a blind date. We had no clue how it would turn out—what if these were horrible, evil people who just wanted to stare and laugh at our imperfect points and improvisational piecing and strange fabric combinations?

But as luck would have it, this is where the two of us first met. We oohed and aahed over each other's show-and-tells. We squealed with delight over new charm packs and jelly rolls. We congratulated and applauded, made suggestions and asked for tips, and talked about a lot of completely non-quilt-related stuff. And friendships were formed at that very first meeting.

And now here we are, just a few short years after that first meeting, having written a book together that celebrates not just our love of quilty deliciousness, but also the community of quilters of which we have been so lucky to become a part. With each passing year, it's obvious that the past is not so distant and the future not so far. So with that said, we hope you enjoy making these quilts inspired by the modern trends we love today and the traditional quilts we cherish from yesterday.

kelly & andie

1 Modern Meets TRADITIONAL

Modern vs. Traditional

You could ask ten different people what the difference is between modern and traditional quilting, and they all would give you a different answer. In general, though, there are a few trends in modern quilting that seem to prevail in most quilts of this genre, as opposed to traditional quilting. This book is built around combining elements from the traditional and modern communities to create quilts that are as representative of our past as they are indicative of our quilting futures.

TRADITIONAL implies:

- Frequent use of multiple borders
- Symmetrical settings and block arrangements
- One-fabric backings
- Mostly neutrals used for backgrounds
- Tan, black and small prints used more than white, gray and solids
- If heavy quilting is used, it's generally employed in a graphic design, like a feather or Baptist fan.
- Elaborate piecing—focus on block design, not fabric design
- Use of quilting cotton exclusively

MODERN means:

- Infrequent use of borders
- Unusual settings and block arrangements, sometimes asymmetrical
- Multiple-fabric pieced backings
- Heavy use of neutrals and solids
- Frequent use of white and gray for backgrounds
- Extremely dense quilting, like a tight stipple or a pebble
- Fairly simple piecing—focus on fabric, not block design
- Use of different kinds of fabrics—quilting cotton, velveteen, linen, muslin, etc.

Like you, we quilt for a variety of reasons. Sometimes, we sew to quiet our minds and escape from the world. Sometimes we sew like crazy to finish a gift quilt or to meet a deadline. And other times we sew to hone our art—because quilting is an art form! The days we have the time and patience to get a little frustrated when it doesn't work the first time are when we should try to expand our understanding of quilting, sewing and our art. So if you're a traditional quilter, try working with a color palette you've never considered, and if you're a modern quilter, tackle a block that intimidates you. Maybe it's just us, but we find there's so much more satisfaction when you successfully make something completely out of your comfort zone.

Perfection and Expression

For the traditional quilter, perfection is the goal: perfectly matched seams, perfectly coordinated fabrics, stunning symmetry and flawless quilting and finishing. Walk through any high-caliber quilt show and the traditional quilts are dripping with perfection. Quilters work for years—decades even—to achieve the kind of construction and finishing that can be considered expert or master level. Both of us are very committed to pushing ourselves to become great sewists and expert quilters since our love of quilting was born from traditional quilts! We love a Double Wedding Ring, a classic 9-Patch or a Drunkard's Path. We respect the rules of traditional quilting because we respect the skill, commitment and time involved in making complicated pieces.

On the flip side, for the modern quilter, the use of unmatched seams, improvisational piecing, negative space, atypical color pairings and asymmetry define the aesthetic of a movement that is often more interested in freedom from the rules of quilting than being bound by them. It's pretty liberating to dive into a pile of fabric with a vague plan and come out on the other side with a finished project that's both useful and beautiful. Quilting as a form of self-expression is a huge factor in the modern scene.

Shunning the rules takes courage for some of us. It can be scary to break the rules, to step outside of those comfy, cozy boundaries of methodical quilting. Rules and order can be soothing and create a zen-like process of cutting, piecing and finishing. Breaking the rules means deliberately tapping into your creativity, pulling out your inner artist and opening yourself up to—dare we say it?—failure. But really, ask yourself this question: What's the worst thing that can happen?

For us, striking a healthy balance between self-expression and being skilled quilters is the goal. Being well-rounded in all areas of quilting elevates your game and allows you to create anything your noggin can dream up, from basic designs to the most mind-blowing pieces.

Modern Art?

Modern quilting is the middle child of traditional quilts and art quilts, wedged between the dutiful older sibling and the wild-child baby of the family.

Modern quilts are made primarily for function. Taking quilts back to their most primitive use while creating an aesthetic that is influenced by architecture, nature, modern art and hints of classic quilt blocks are what set modern quilts apart from art quilts.

Art quilts are typically made with a mixed-media focus, meaning that non-fabric elements and embellishments, avant-garde motifs and non-traditional finishing are heavily used. Art quilts are of the classification of function following way behind form. While we both admire art quilters and their sense of adventure and boundary pushing, we love a crinkly, cottony, quilty gem wrapped around our shoulders.

7

Fabric and Color

Choosing fabric can be the most difficult part of quilting for many people. In the modern movement, it is perfectly acceptable to combine modern graphic prints with reproduction fabrics, to use solids with solids, and to use upcycled/vintage fabrics (even if they're not 100-percent cotton). Modern quilters use linens and cottons and velveteens in their creations, and the results will be different than using quilter's cotton.

There are many different ways to choose fabrics, but they're not all creative and they won't all give the result you want. Rather than running down the list of materials needed for a particular quilt, really look at the pattern and decide how you want your version to look. Maybe make a sample block or do a color sketch to try out some new options. Think of our quilts as a suggestion—a jumping-off point. Then, make it yours.

A great way to choose fabrics for a quilt is to find one fabric that you absolutely love—one with great colors and images, lots of interest. Then, find fabrics that go with your inspiration fabric, playing with and building upon the color palette that exists in the main fabric. Pull solids and repros and small prints and large prints—anything that goes with the first fabric. And then—get rid of the first fabric! What you're left with is a group of fabrics that play together brilliantly, but you may never have considered putting together. You can see this fabric selection technique used in the **Urban Cabin Quilt** (page 78).

Most importantly, remember that there isn't a right or wrong way to combine fabrics. If you like it, then it's beautiful. If you hate it, then put it back on the shelf. Too often, we let trends determine how we combine fabrics and we stop listening to our gut. Well, start listening! Your fabric gut is almost never wrong.

Curating Your Fabric Stash

Every quilter builds their stash differently. We happen to buy what we like when we see it, especially when it's piled on the remnant cart at our favorite quilting emporium. Some of us are need-based buyers, buying only what we need for a specific

project. Some of us inherit fabric and some of us compulsively buy it, justifying it all the way home. Building your stash should be a very deliberate act—buying fabric that you kinda like and you think needs a home will only result in fabric that takes up space and eventually will be given away.

However you fill your stash, it's important to buy quality, well-made fabrics. A dense weave and saturated color will make your quilts last longer and give you a more professional, polished piece.

The ultimate goal is to have a good supply of basics that can blend with and be mixed with other basics to create a pleasing palette. Whether you prefer geometrics or florals, novelty prints or Civil War reproductions, buy what you know you'll use.

There's also a current trend in upcycling and repurposing vintage and garment fabrics. A baby quilt made from men's cotton dress shirts backed with a vintage sheet screams modern quilt. Thrift stores, antique stores and rummage sales can yield some yummy fabric scores, like feedsacks and mid-century modern remnants, for a vintage-licious bundle of fabric for your stash.

Most importantly, buy what you love, whether it's polka dots and florals, or a wacky, offbeat print. If you see it and fall in love with it and it's something that you know you'll use eventually, take it home with you.

Seeking Out Your People

Quilting is a solitary sport, which is part of its appeal. You can hole up with a cup of coffee, turn up the music and just sew. There's no need to talk, no need to play nice with others, no need to pass the ball. The solitude of quilting can be absolutely glorious.

But because of the built-in solitude of quilting, it's that much more important to seek out your people—the gals and guys who freak out about fabric and patterns like you do.

Just like with any hobby or interest, it's so fun to find friends who understand why you love what you love. You will find support, encouragement, suggestions and honesty among the people who love all things quilty. So don't get so enraptured by the solitude that you forget you need the "oohs and aahs!"

Check in your surrounding area for quilt guilds or small sewing groups you can join. If there isn't one, start one! Check out the Modern Quilt Guild website (see *Resources* on page 125) for a list of current branches and information on how to start your own.

And remember that you can connect virtually even easier. Communities are popping up every day online to support groups of quilters and sewists, giving them a platform to display their work and to learn from others. Just start double-clicking—you'll find quilt friends all over the world from the comfort of your own home.

Making Friends With Technology

Learning to sew online and building a worldwide sewing circle are two of the most influential trends in quilting today. You can learn to sew just by visiting blogs, watching videos, becoming a member of an online quilting board, and taking advantage of the free patterns that fabric companies offer. There's really no substitute for taking a class with a real, live quilting professional, but for those who want to learn the basics of quilting, the Internet is an amazing place to be educated.

Exposure to such a huge body of work is a tremendous gift to us quilters. We can hop online, visit quilters literally all over the world and take a peek into what they're working on, what fabric they're using, what technique they're learning and what shows they've attended. Being able to connect to quilters in Australia, France and Japan, for us, has been a ginormous influence. And making friends through social network sites like Twitter, Flickr and Facebook, along with our favorite quilting boards, makes us feel connected and helps keep our creativity fresh. How amazing is it that your sewing circle can have such an international flair?

If We Can, You Can

We, my friends, are not quilting gurus. We experiment, we rip, we break needles. Our points aren't always perfect, sometimes our seams are not a perfect quarter-inch, and occasionally we

want to throw our sewing machines out the window and take up badminton.

We confess all of these sewing crimes because we want you to be brave and feel confident enough to make any quilt you want. It may not be perfect. You may have to rip or start over or scream into a pillow for awhile, but ultimately you can do it! Believe us, we didn't just sit down and sew up these quilts in a weekend. They were a total challenge for us, but we did it—and hopefully our instructions will help you avoid some of the frustration and just skip right to the successful ending.

Long story short: If we can do it, you can do it! Because we aren't quilting gurus—we're just two girls who like quarter-inch seams, delicious fabric and the feel of a quilt around our shoulders.

2 The TECHNIQUES

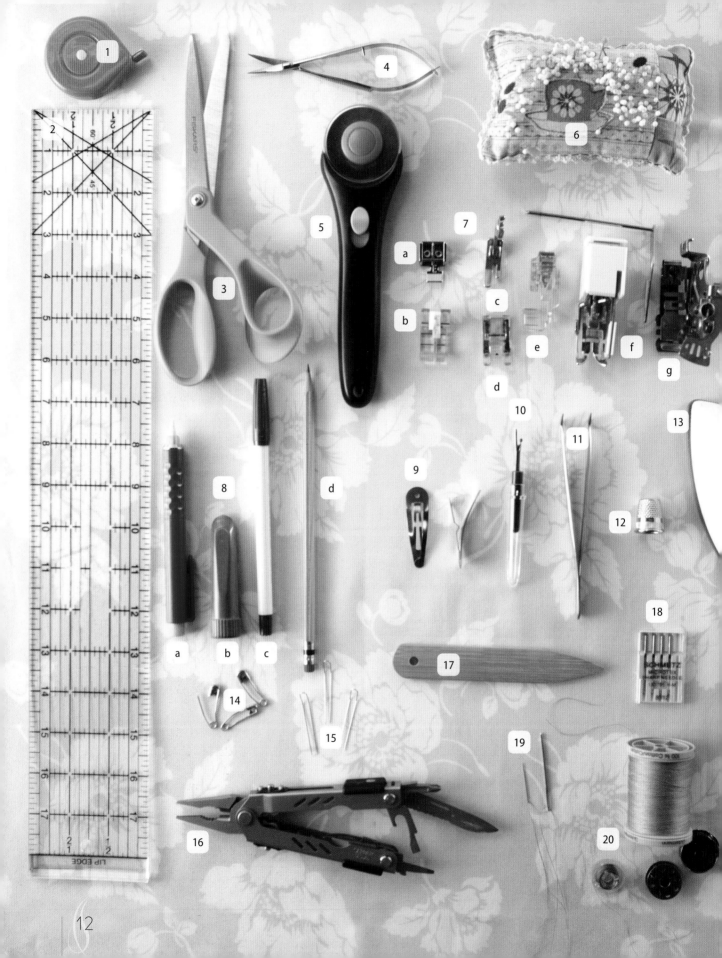

Stuff to Get

1. **Flexible tape measure:** Necessary for measuring quilt widths or other long lengths (or around curves, like a waist).
2. **Acrylic quilter's rectangular ruler:** We recommend a 24" (70cm) long rectangular ruler for cutting across the width of fabric (when folded, approximately 22" [55.9cm]), and a shorter one for subcutting strips.
3. **Fabric scissors:** Get some good scissors, and use them for fabric cutting only. Paper will dull the blades.
4. **Snips:** Perfect to keep next to your machine to snip threads.
5. **Rotary cutter:** Use this tool to cut and subcut strips. Use it only with a rotary cutting mat (not shown), and be careful to keep your fingers out of the way.
6. **Pins and pincushion:** There are lots of different pins, but for most piecing we recommend fine-point pins with a ball or flower head. And you can never have too many pincushions!
7. **Machine feet:** There's a foot for everything! Start growing your collection and you'll love the different results you can achieve. Shown are: (a) zipper foot, (b) ¼" (6mm) clear foot, (c) narrow foot, (d) appliqué foot, (e) freemotion/hopping foot, (f) walking foot with guide bar and (g) ruffler foot.
8. **Marking tools:** There are lots of marking tools to use on fabric. Try a few to find the one you like best. Shown are: (a) chalk pen, (b) chalk wheel, (c) evaporating fabric marker and (d) standard pencil.
9. **Hair clips:** Available at any drugstore, these snap-in-place clips are great for holding binding in place as you stitch it to the back of your quilt.
10. **Seam ripper:** We all know what this is for. And unfortunately, we will all need it from time to time. Let's move on…
11. **Tweezers:** Excellent for removing snippets of thread or basting stitches.
12. **Thimble:** You may find one uncomfortable at first, but it's better than a sore finger.
13. **Iron:** Invest in a good, really hot iron that can be used with or without steam. An automatic shut-off is a nice feature.
14. **Curved safety pins:** These pins are slightly curved on the bottom, making it easier to scoop them through three quilt layers when basting.
15. **Fork pins:** These are very fine double-pronged pins. See Andie's method for pinning intersecting seams on page 19 using these pins.
16. **Multi-tool:** Sewing machines are just that—machines. Sometimes we need to get in there with pliers or a screwdriver. Make sure you have a multi-tool or basic tools handy just in case.
17. **Turning tool:** Great for turning out points, like on Dresden wedges or pillow corners. Just prod gently…
18. **Sewing machine needles:** Change out your machine's needle frequently—certainly every time you start a new, big project. The needle will become dull and your machine simply won't sew as well as it could.
19. **Hand sewing needles:** A fine, flexible needle is needed for sewing on binding or appliqué, but a sturdier needle is better for tying a quilt.
20. **Thread and bobbins:** Be sure to choose good quality thread, whether it's a poly blend or 100-percent cotton, and stock up when you can on a variety of colors for quilting and appliqué. Gray, white, beige and black threads are usually sufficient for any piecing. Wind those bobbins ahead of time! There's nothing worse than having to stop sewing over and over to refill the bobbin.

Quilter's spray starch

Using quilter's spray starch (see Resources on page 125) on finished blocks can help smooth out minor problem areas. It is also great to use on fabric pieces before you sew, because the stiffness helps keep small fabric pieces from stretching out of shape as they go through your machine.

Techniques to Know

Cutting, Sewing and Pressing

A lot of quilting problems can be averted early on by taking the time to cut and sew precisely. Luckily, even when we do get in a rush, some errors can be rectified with a little fancy pressing.

 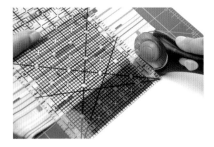 

1 Always begin with a new straight edge. Before cutting strips, squares or any straight-edge shape, always square off the edge of your fabric. Even if you think it's straight, cut a new edge anyway.

2 When cutting strips, be sure to cut the strips so that they are at a perfect 90-degree angle with the folded or bottom edge of the fabric. If the strips are not perfectly square to the fold, when you open the strip, there will be a wave at the fold.

Don't cut toward you
Never, ever, ever cut toward yourself or under your arm. Not only is it unsafe, your fabric cuts won't be accurate.

What is WOF?
If you see the abbreviation WOF, this stands for width of fabric, meaning the measurement from one selvage to the other (approximately 42" [106.7cm]).

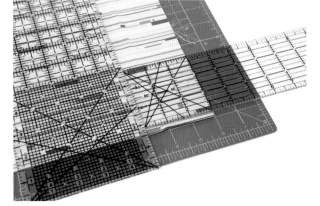

3 Your rotary cutting mat and rulers have measurements and straight lines on them for a reason. Use them all to make sure that each time you cut, you wind up with a perfectly cut piece of fabric. If your fabric isn't accurate at this stage, it's certainly not going to be accurate after you sew it.

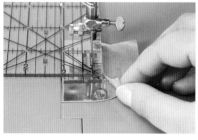

SEWING A ¼" (6MM) SEAM

Measure, mark and test your ¼" (6mm) seam. From the needle, measure over ¼" (6mm). Mark this point on your machine bed with a piece of painter's tape. This tape gives you a guideline for sewing a perfect ¼" (6mm) seam. Be sure to test this mark. Sew two scrap pieces together, and then measure the seam allowance. Adjust the tape marking as necessary.

DON'T BE AFRAID TO RIP

It's always better to rip and re-sew than to be pulling and tugging blocks to line up down the road.

PRESSING SEAMS TO THE SIDE

When pressing seams to the side, press toward the darker fabric unless instructed otherwise in the pattern. This keeps the underlying seam from shadowing through lighter fabrics.

PRESSING SEAMS OPEN

If the point where a lot of seams intersect isn't looking as crisp as you'd like, try pressing the seam open instead of to the side.

PRESS IT FLAT

If your block is bubbling in the center or is a little small—press, press, press! Always press from the center out to each corner and each side to avoid stretching the fabrics out of shape.

Test it out

Make test blocks to figure out trouble spots early. Some blocks and designs need a little extra TLC, and it's much better to find out how to sew a tricky one with scrap fabric instead of the super-gorgeous stuff you just bought. And frankly, you might decide after your test block is finished that you absolutely hated making it and have no desire to turn it into a king-size bed quilt. Better to find out early rather than after you've bought all the fabric.

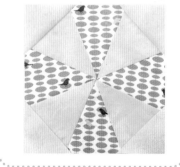

Squaring Up a Block

Few tasks in quilt-making are as dreaded as this one. You've finally pieced a set of beautiful, delicious blocks and all you want to do is sew them together and finish your quilt. But slow down, friend. Sewing together unsquared blocks is a surefire way to get a wonky, wavy quilt with seams that don't line up. Take a breath, dig deep for some patience and finish strong.

What size should my block be?

Some patterns may not indicate what size to square your block. In this case, look for the "unfinished block size," which is the size of the block with a ¼" (6mm) seam allowance on all four sides. Don't square to a "finished block size"—that is the size after the blocks are sewn next to each other, and after the ¼" (6mm) seam allowance has been taken out.

1 Triple-check the size you should be trimming the blocks. Then mark the lines on a large square ruler with painter's tape so there's no way you'll cut your block too small. The worst thing would be to cut off your ¼" (6mm) seam allowances in this process, so check, check, check before cutting!

2 Now that the block has been pieced, the interior seams are what you need to align your ruler with—not the outside edges. If your block has a definite center point, mark the center of the square on your ruler so you can be sure the center point is the actual center of your trimmed block. Take the time to really adjust your block under the ruler.

3 Cut along one side and the top of the ruler, holding the ruler firmly in place.

4 Rotate the block 180 degrees and align the markings on the ruler with the edges you just cut. Holding the ruler firmly in place, cut along the final two sides of the ruler. Your block should now be a perfectly sized square.

Manipulating Stripes

Striped fabric can be extremely versatile, depending on how you cut it and sew it. Experiment with stripes in practice blocks to see how different cutting and sewing methods can quickly turn a striped print into an optical illusion.

Stripes are great to use in stand-alone blocks or pieced next to different prints. The only challenge when using stripes in this way is making sure to cut the stripes straight. Sometimes fabrics aren't printed perfectly parallel or perpendicular to the grain. With a tossed or allover print, this usually isn't noticeable, but with a stripe it definitely will be.

CUTTING STRAIGHT STRIPES

If the stripe isn't perfectly parallel or perpendicular to the fabric grain, open your fabric to its full width to cut. Then, cut strips perfectly even with or perpendicular to the stripe, not with the straight of grain. (If you cut off grain with the fabric folded, you will have a wave in the strip when you unfold it.) If your mat isn't long enough, cut, then slide the fabric up and cut again. **Note:** If your stripe isn't even with the straight of grain, buy about ¼ yard (.2m) more fabric than you think you will need to allow for any fabric that will be lost in cutting.

ROTATION

This sounds simple, but bear in mind that your stripes have a directionality—they can either run vertically across your quilt or horizontally. Keep this in mind as you use them in a quilt, or you may wind up with a block or two that differs from the others. Stripes running in both directions appear in the *Urban Cabin Quilt* on page 78.

CUTTING BIAS STRIPES

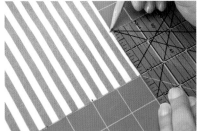

1 Cutting bias stripes eats up a lot of fabric, but the effect can really be worth it. Stripes cut on the bias create a barbershop-pole effect on your quilt, which adds a lot of movement. Bias-cut stripes are particularly nice for narrow borders and bindings. To cut bias strips, open your fabric flat (unfolded). From the bottom right corner, measure and mark over 2" (5.1cm) and up 2" (5.1cm).

2 Cut a diagonal line connecting these points. Cut strips even with this first cut line at the desired width until you have created enough strips to use for your project. Piece them end to end to create strips long enough to use, matching up the stripes to the best of your ability.

Matching Straight Seams (Kelly's Method)

Much to my mother's dismay, I resisted pinning for the longest time. Pinning all those seams took forever, and it seemed like such a waste of time! But just like Mom said I would, I discovered that ripping and re-sewing takes a much longer time than pinning does. You'll want to use these techniques (or Andie's, depending on which you prefer) any time you have seams that need to intersect when sewn together.

press

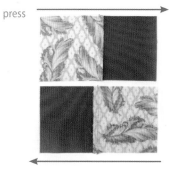

press

1 When seams on two different sections of your quilt need to intersect when sewn together, press the seams in opposite directions.

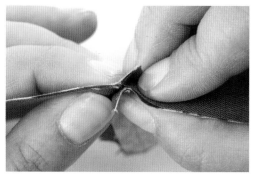

2 Place the pieces right sides together, as you will be sewing them. Wiggle the intersecting seams together with your fingers; you will feel them butt up next to each other.

3 Peek inside the seam allowance to double-check that the seams are intersecting.

4 Place a pin directly through the seam intersection to hold the seams in place.

5 Sew the seam, removing the pin just before you reach it, and then continuing to sew gingerly over the seam intersection.

Kelly says...

When sewing long rows together, there may be many seams that intersect and need to be aligned. Nest and pin every single one on this way. If your piecing wasn't perfect when stitching the rows, you can still ease the intersections to align at this phase by pinning and then gently stretching the fabrics to your will. Just make them line up as you sew.

Matching Straight Seams (Andie's Method)

← press →

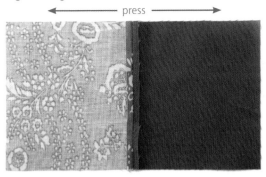

1 Press the seams open. I prefer to press my seams open as opposed to pressing them to one side. I do this for a few reasons: (1) I like that the seams and corners lay much flatter, and (2) I'm not very good at keeping track of which way to iron so my seams match up later. With some blocks, though, like curved blocks, pressing open isn't possible.

2 Line up the seams of both pieces so they match. You will be able to see from the raw edge if they are aligned.

3 Place a fork pin through the top piece and through to the back, straddling the seams evenly with both points.

4 Bring the fork pin points back through the back piece through to the front, repeating the straddling of points like you did on the front, making sure they are aligned with the seams.

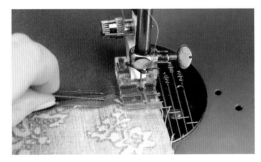

5 These pins are superfine, so if you're fearless enough, you can sew right over them. I'm a chicken and don't really like to sew over pins, so I sew to the first point, needle down, and pull the fork pin back far enough to get it out of the way of the needle, but still securing the seam.

Andie says...

I like to use a little tool called fork pins. They are helpful when lining up seams and ensuring a nice finished corner. They can be found in most large-chain fabric stores and online quilt shops. These pins work best when you place the tines very close to the seam.

Matching Diagonal Seams

Anytime you have two diagonally sewn seams come together, you're going to have a little extra work to make sure they intersect properly. Unlike straight seams, diagonal seams won't intersect at the edge of the fabric—they have to intersect ¼" (6mm) inside the edge, or where the stitches will fall. This technique will make sure your diagonal seams intersect beautifully the first time around.

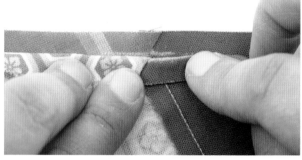

1 It sounds simple, but identify the two diagonal seams that need to intersect. With a ruler and a chalk marker, carefully measure and mark the ¼" (6mm) seam across both seams.

2 Place the pieces right sides together. Peel back the edge of the top fabric and carefully place the drawn ¼" (6mm) seam lines on top of one another. Once the ¼" (6mm) seam markings are aligned, scoot the top fabric into position so that, at the drawn ¼" (6mm) line, the two diagonal seams intersect.

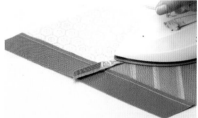

4 Stitch over the intersection with a ¼" (6mm) seam. Press the seam.

3 Carefully pin the intersection and at several other places before and after the intersection.

Joining across borders

If you are joining diagonal seams across a border or sashing, as you do in the Must Stash Quilt (page 100), simply extend the diagonal seam with chalk across the sashing, and mark the ¼" (6mm) seam line as before. This will ensure that, even though the diagonal seams don't touch, they are still perfectly in line with one another across the quilt top.

Sewing Curved Seams

Sewing a curved seam is a technique that intimidates a lot of quilters. But fear not! Curved seams just take a little patience and practice. This is a technique that, once mastered, will open up new possibilities in your sewing and impress even the most experienced quilters.

1 Fold each piece in half and finger press the fold to mark the middle. Or, mark the center of each piece with a chalk pencil. Start with both pieces lying together as they will look when they are sewn together.

2 Pin the midpoints of the curves right sides together. Do this by keeping Piece 2 in place, right side facing up, and flipping Piece 1 over on top of Piece 2 so that it's wrong side up and the midpoint of its inner curve meets the midpoint of Piece 2's outer curve.

3 Begin in the center and, working your way to the right, pin every inch or so, with the pin head facing away from the curve.

4 Sew with a ¼" (6mm) seam around the curved edge, carefully making sure that the seams are smooth and pucker-free.

5 Cut little notches in the seam every ½" (12mm) or so to ease the tension in the seam.

6 With a dry iron, press toward the bow of the curve.

Paper Piecing

Paper piecing is one of the surest ways to achieve accuracy. This technique does take some practice, as it's sometimes hard to get the hang of literally working backwards when piecing the block. When sewing, use a shorter stitch than you normally would use when piecing. This will perforate the paper and make removing it much easier. Usually, paper-piecing patterns are numbered, which makes it easy to follow along. Think of it as sewing-by-number!

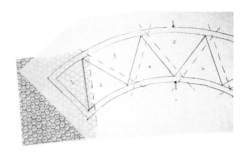

1 Begin by placing the first fabric piece on the template—on the unprinted side of the paper—over Space 1, with the right side facing out and the raw edges extending ¼" (6mm) (to the dotted line) past the border lines printed on the other side. This may require a light box, a window or a light that will help you see through the paper and line everything up.

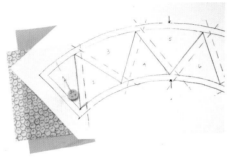

2 Place the second piece of fabric (the one that will cover the second space) right sides together over the first piece. Match the raw edges. Pin the fabrics in place through the paper.

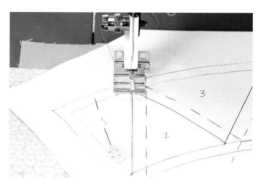

3 Place the paper/fabric under the presser foot on your sewing machine, carefully lining up the needle with the solid line between Space 1 and Space 2.

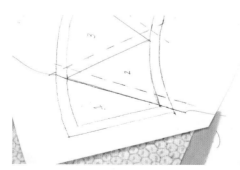

4 Sew along the line and through the seam allowances with a short stitch, backstitching at the beginning and end of the seam. This makes the seam more secure when the paper is torn off later.

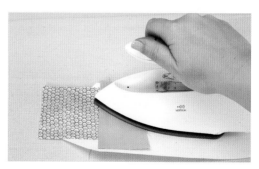

5 Flip Piece 2 open, and press it flat with a dry iron.

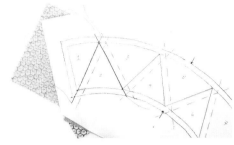

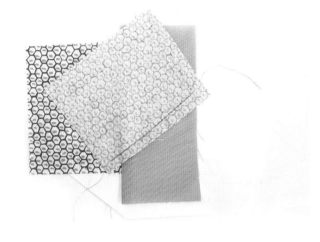

6 Add Piece 3 (photos show front and back).

7 Trim the seam to ¼" (6mm), making sure to flip the paper back and out of the way before trimming.

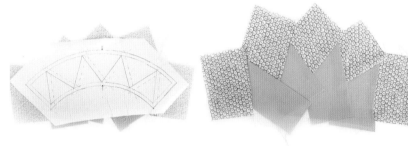

8 Continue to add each piece, matching edges, sewing along the lines and trimming and pressing pieces until you have covered all of the spaces (photos show front and back).

9 Using the pattern edges as a guide, trim off the excess fabric and paper, being careful to be as exact as possible. *Note:* Before trimming, look to see if your paper-piecing pattern includes a ¼" (6mm) seam allowance on all sides. If it does, you can trim even with the edge of the paper pattern. If it doesn't, you'll need to trim the block ¼" (6mm) wider on all sides than the paper pattern.

10 Gently tear the paper away from the back of each pieced unit.

English Paper-Piecing Hexies

Whipping together these little hexie gems takes only minutes and they're totally portable, which means you can get oodles of them done while waiting out downtime at doctors' offices, the kiddos' soccer practice or watching TV. It really only takes making one to get the hang of the technique, and after only a few, you'll develop your own methods.

Use a good-quality cotton thread to shape the hexies, and try invisible thread for joining them. Invisible thread isn't the easiest stuff to work with, but the finished product is well worth the extra effort.

Invisible thread

1 For one hexie, cut out or buy a paper hexagon template. Cut out one hexie from paper. Then cut a square of fabric that is 1" (2.5cm) larger than your paper hexie. Pin the paper hexie to the center of the wrong side of the fabric square.

2 Fold over the right top side of the fabric followed by the top side. If you are left-handed, do the opposite (do the left followed by the top).

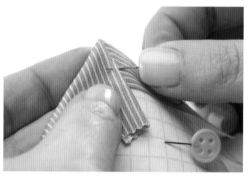

3 Beginning on the folded corner, place the needle in the fabric, going from right to left (or left to right), making sure to push the needle through both flaps of fabric but not the paper.

4 Pull the needle through, leaving a tail about 1½" (3.8cm) long.

5 Repeat step 4 by making another stitch in the same spot (backstitch).

6 Move to the next corner. Repeat steps 2–6 for the rest of the corners, except the last one.

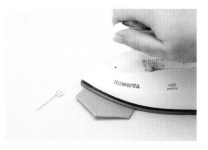

7 Tuck the final corner in the same direction as the rest.

8 Knot off when the hexie is complete.

9 Remove the center pin and press the hexie with a dry iron, but don't remove the paper yet.

10 To join hexies, place two hexies right sides together and whipstitch along one edge, stitching both hexies together. Be careful not to sew into the paper piece in the middle. (Not a lot of stitches are necessary. For a 3" [7.6cm] hexie, use 8–10 stitches per side.) *Note:* Even tension on the stitches will prevent them from showing through to the front. For demo purposes, invisible thread was not used here.

11 Knot off when you reach the end of a hexie cluster; if moving into a corner, continue to the next seam.

12 Keep adding pieces and repeating the previous steps until the desired shape is achieved (a row, flower cluster, pyramid, etc.).

13 Remove the paper pieces from the centers, and reuse them in your next hexie project. Appliqué the hexie shapes to a quilt block using a zigzag, straight or blanket stitch. Or, piece the hexies into one large block to make a quilt top.

Installing a Zipper

Whether you're making home decorating projects, bags and purses or a garment, a zipper adds a practical and professional touch. There are several different types of zippers, and they come in a rainbow of colors and range in length from 5 inches (12.7cm) to 10 feet (3m) long (for items like sleeping bags). Most zippers are made from polyester webbing that has either plastic or metal teeth and a zipper pull. Zippers are readily available in fabric stores and online shops, and specialty zippers can be ordered straight from the manufacturer.

To make installation easier, a zipper foot on your sewing machine is ideal. And because we're stitching from the inside out, your bobbin thread should match the fabric. Here, we'll show you how to install a zipper in a pillow, but these techniques can be used for a variety of zipper projects.

Zipper foot

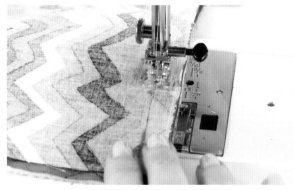

1 Sew a ½" (12mm) seam where the zipper will be installed, using a longer stitch (a basting stitch) than normal.

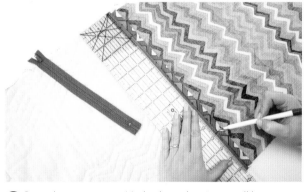

2 Press the seam open. Mark where the zipper will be centered on the seam, equidistant from each end of the pillow.

3 Close the zipper. Align the zipper facedown on the seam, with the back facing up. Pin it in place.

4 Start sewing on the end where the zipper pull is. With the zipper foot attached, sew along the zipper teeth, being very careful to sew as close to the teeth as possible without sewing into them.

5 When you get to the end of the zipper teeth, put your needle down and pivot the seam perpendicular to the foot; sew along the end of the zipper, again being careful to avoid the teeth or stopper. Reinforce the stopper end by reverse stitching over the seam.

6 Pivot and sew up the other side of the zipper like you did in step 4.

7 When you get to the top, remove the project from the machine. With a seam ripper, remove the basting stitches from the middle of the zipper to the stopper-end stitching.

8 Pull the zipper pull down away from the end very gently about 3" (7.6cm). This will make it easier to sew the end of the zipper. Place the project back under the zipper foot and sew like you did in step 5.

9 Using the seam ripper, open up the rest of the seam and clean up any little threads with a pair of tweezers. Finish the pillow by leaving the zipper open for turning and sewing along the other sides to close. Turn out and fill with the pillow form.

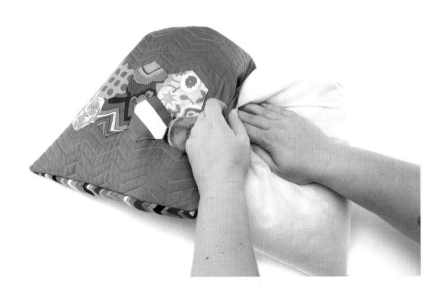

Ruffling

Find your ruffler foot in the bottom of your drawer and get to be friends. Sure, it looks terrifyingly complex, but once you know how to use it, it's not only easy but extremely satisfying to turn a strip of fabric into a frilly ruffle.

Ruffler foot

setting 12 ruffle

setting 6 ruffle

setting 1 ruffle

Do the math before you start

1. First, determine the length of ruffles you need, and add about 6" (15.2cm) to that number for some wiggle room. For example, if you need 6" (15.2cm) of ruffles, plan to make 12" (30.5cm) of ruffles to be on the safe side.

2. Since creating ruffles scrunches up the cut length of fabric, you will need to start with more fabric than determined in step 1 above. Most ruffler feet also have an adjustment screw that allows you to increase or decrease the length of the space between ruffles; the stitch length you set also affects the length between ruffles. Use a medium stitch length. If you will be using your ruffler foot on the "1" setting, multiply the number from step 1 by 3. If using the "6" setting, multiply by 2, and for the "12" setting, multiply by 1½.

For example, if you need 12" (30.5cm) of ruffles using the "1" setting, you will need to start with about 36" (91.4cm) of fabric.

Note: Since every machine is different, the most accurate method is to do a ruffle swatch. Using the setting you want and the stitch length you want, ruffle a 12" (30.5cm) swatch of fabric, and measure the amount of ruffles produced. Use this as a determination for how much extra fabric to cut before making your real ruffle.

RUFFLE TYPES

On most ruffler feet, there are three settings: 12, 6 and 1. This means that the foot will make a tuck to create a ruffle every 12 stitches, every 6 stitches or every single stitch. A tuck every 12 stitches will produce a very wide ruffle, and a tuck every single stitch will make a very dense, frilly ruffle.

Improvise a ruffle

If you don't have a ruffler foot, simply sew a long basting stitch down the edge of your folded strip. Then, gather or cinch the thread to create a ruffled effect.

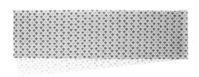

1 Cut and piece a 5" (12.7cm) wide strip of fabric the length you need (see page 28). (*Note:* You can use a strip wider or narrower depending on the width of the ruffle you want. 5" [12.7cm] is a good width to use for practice.) Using the example, we will be cutting a 5" × 36"(12.7cm × 91.4cm) strip of fabric.

2 Fold and press the strip in half lengthwise with wrong sides together, matching the raw edges.

3 Starting at one end of the folded strip, with the raw edges to the right, slip the end under the middle tong of the ruffler foot. Pull the strip firmly underneath the metal clip and to the right to really secure it into the foot.

4 Pull a few inches (centimeters) of the strip through the back of the foot, so there is fabric under the needle and enough for you to hold onto behind the foot. Put your presser foot down. Begin stitching, using both hands to hold the strip in the groove of the foot. The foot will do the rest of the job for you.

5 Remove your ruffles and be amazed! Sew the ruffle strip into an unfinished seam by sandwiching the ruffles inside two pieces of fabrics that are placed right sides together. Align the raw edges. Stitch along the raw edge with a ¼" (6mm) seam. When you open the fabrics up, the ruffle will be stitched in the middle. You can apply this technique to a variety of projects, including the ruffled binding used on the *La Femme de la Mer Quilt* on page 75.

Raw-Edge Appliqué

There are a variety of ways to appliqué (or apply) one piece of fabric directly onto another piece of fabric. In our opinion, this way is the easiest.

1 Cut out a piece of fabric that is a bit larger all around than the size of your appliqué shape. Following the manufacturer's instructions, fuse double-sided fusible web to the wrong side of the fabric. Don't remove the paper backing yet.

2 Trace the outline of the appliqué onto the paper backing of the fusible web. Keep in mind that you need to trace the mirror image of the design you ultimately want. Cut out the appliqué shape from the fabric and fusible web. Remove the paper backing.

3 With a hot iron, fuse the appliqué shape in place. Stitch around the outside of the shape using the thread of your choice. Straight stitch close to the edge, or use a satin stitch (a zigzag stitch with a short stitch length, so the zigzags lie next to each other) to completely cover the raw edges.

Tying a Quilt

There are two ways to secure the layers of a quilt: quilting and tying. Quilting secures the layers together by sewing through all three layers of the quilt, often adding a decorative element with the stitches. Tying is much simpler and quicker to do, and adds a more rustic appearance to the quilt.

1 Layer your quilt sandwich as normal, flattening and smoothing all of the layers well. Baste your quilt with quilting safety pins or basting spray. You won't need to baste as thoroughly as you would for machine quilting, but still baste thoroughly to avoid slippage.

2 Cut a long piece (about 6 feet [1.8m]) of coordinating/contrasting embroidery floss. Thread all six strands through the eye of a large needle (tapestry needles work well). The centers or intersections of blocks are usually good places for your knots, which should be no further than a fist width's apart from each other. At your first point, stitch down through all three layers, leaving a 3" (7.6cm) floss tail on top of the quilt.

3 Stitch back up through all three layers right next to the entrance point. Cut the thread to leave another 3" (7.6cm) tail. Tie the two floss tails together in a knot, pulling tight but not hard enough to pucker or rip the fabric. Tie two more knots to secure the floss. Trim the tails short. Continue stitching and tying in this way, rethreading your needle when necessary, until you have tied the entire quilt.

3 The PROJECTS

FLYING GEESE QUILT
In the Clouds

by Andie

The use of negative space in modern quilting is an important element in breaking the rules of symmetry and balance. For this quilt, I took one large, off-centered flying geese block and used it to create a Swedish-inspired design that is minimalist in attitude. The navy blue background was used to create negative space, but more specifically it mimics water. It's as if we're sitting on a cloud looking down, watching the geese fly over a pristine lake or river.

FINISHED SIZE:	81¾" × 95"
	(201.6cm × 241.2cm)
LEVEL:	Beginner
QUILTED BY:	Jill Montgomery

Materials

7½ yards (6.9m) of solid navy blue fabric (background, binding)

33 assorted pieces/scraps of geometric prints, each at least 6¼" (15.9cm) square (geese)

7⅝ yards (6.9m) of standard-width fabric or 3 yards (2.7m) of 90" (228.6cm) wide fabric (backing)

Batting

Thread

Other

Template (page 122)

Template plastic

Basic quilting/sewing tools

Cutting

From the navy fabric, cut:

- Panel 1: WOF × 95" (WOF × 241.2cm)
- Panel 2: 20½" × 46" (52.1cm × 116.9cm)
- Panel 3: 20½" × 22" (52.1cm × 55.9cm)
- Panel 4: 23" × 95" (58.4cm × 241.3cm)
- (2) 3" × 28" (7.6cm × 71.1cm) strips
- (3) WOF × 4" (8.9cm) strips; subcut each strip into 4" (8.9cm) squares, then cut each square once diagonally to make a total of 66 background triangles

From 33 different assorted fabric scraps, cut 33 main printed triangles using the template (page 122)

Make the Flying Geese and Geese Panel

For each "goose," you'll need 1 print triangle and 2 navy triangles.

1. With right sides together, center the bottom of a navy background triangle over the side of a main printed triangle (Figure 1).

2. Sew along the edge with a ¼" (6mm) seam allowance. Flip the navy piece open and press, with the seam allowance toward the navy side (Figure 2).

3. Repeat to sew a navy triangle to the left side of the printed triangle (Figure 3).

4. Trim the resulting block to 3" × 5½" (7.6cm × 14cm), making sure you have at least a ¼" (6mm) seam allowance above the point of the triangle (Figure 4).

5. Repeat steps 1–4 to make a total of 33 geese units.

6. Arrange the geese into 3 columns, each column with 11 geese units. Geese in the outside columns should point north, and geese in the center column should point south. Sew the units together into 3 columns.

7. Sew a 3" × 28" (7.6cm × 71.1cm) navy strip to each side of the center, south-facing column to create the center unit.

8. Sew a north-facing outside column to both sides of the center unit (Figure 5). This completes the geese panel.

Figure 1

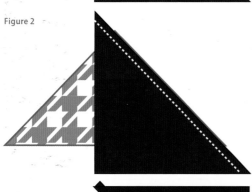

Figure 2

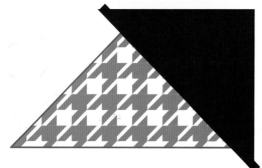

Figure 3

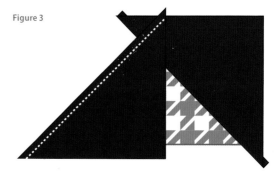

Figure 4

Assemble and Finish the Quilt

Follow the Layout Diagram to assemble the quilt, made of 4 solid navy panels and the geese panel.

1. Sew Panel 2 to the top of the geese panel.

2. Sew Panel 3 to the bottom of the geese panel. You now have one long panel, with the geese block in the middle.

3. Sew Panel 1 to the left side of the geese panel, being sure to sew as straight a seam as possible.

4. Sew Panel 4 to the right side of the geese panel, again sewing a very straight seam.

5. Layer the quilt top with backing and batting, and then baste and quilt. The quilting was done in a heavy ripple pattern to mirror the feeling of water.

6. Finish by binding with the remaining navy fabric, in 2½" (6.3cm) wide strips.

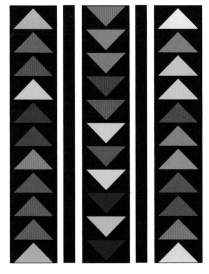

Figure 5

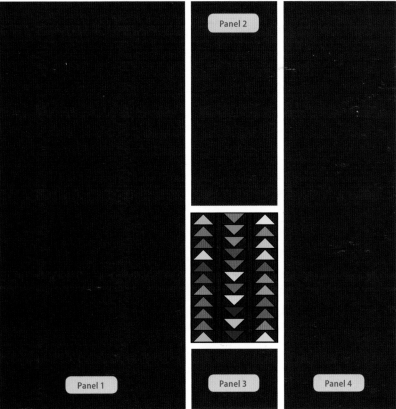

Layout Diagram

IN THE CLOUDS QUILT

MINI-PROJECT
Placemats

by Andie

I scored this vintage floral fabric during a girls' weekend in
Chicago. It was piled under a heap of 1950s unfinished quilt
tops that, to this day, I could kick myself for not buying at
least two or three of. Because this fabric is slightly busy, it
makes for good background fabric for these geese, as it helps to
hide the seams.

FINISHED SIZE:	12" × 17"
	(30.5cm × 43.2cm)
LEVEL:	Beginner

Materials
(for 4 placemats)

¼ yard (.2m) or fat quarter (geese)

1½ yards (1.4m) of fabric (background, binding)

⅞ yard (.9m) of fabric (backing)

(4) 15" × 20" (38.1cm × 50.8cm) pieces of batting

Thread

Other
Disappearing pen or pencil

Basic quilting/sewing tools

Cutting
From the background fabric, cut:

- (16) 3⅛" (7.9cm) squares
- Panel A: (4) 2½" × 12" (6.4cm × 30.5cm) strips
- Panels B and C: (8) 5" × 1¾" (12.7cm × 4.4cm) rectangles
- Panel D: (4) 10½" × 12" (26.7cm × 30.5cm) rectangles

From the geese fabric, cut (4) 5¾" (14.6cm) squares

Figure 1

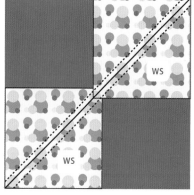

Make the Geese

1. Using a disappearing pen or pencil, draw a diagonal line on the wrong side of each of the (16) 3⅛" (7.9cm) background squares.

2. Start with one 5¾" (14.6cm) geese square, right side up. Place and pin 2 background squares in opposite corners of the geese fabric, right sides together, so that the diagonal line is matching. The interior corners of the background squares will overlap slightly. Sew a ¼" (6mm) seam on either side of the marked line (Figure 1).

3. Cut along the drawn line. You will now have 2 pieces. Open the small triangles and iron the seam allowances toward the background fabric (Figure 2). Set one piece aside.

Figure 2

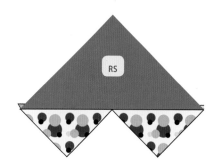

Andie says…
Mixing vintage fabrics like feedsacks and antique bed sheets with modern solids and prints is a very gratifying way of making something old new again. Being able to fuse different eras together in one project is a skill both Kelly and I try very hard to master.

4. With right sides together and the marked line running from corner to center, place a 3⅛" (7.9cm) background square in the corner of one of the pieces. Sew a ¼" (6mm) seam along each side of the marked line (Figure 3). Repeat with the other piece from step 3.

5. Cut along the diagonal marked line on both pieces, creating 4 geese units (Figure 4). Flip the background fabric open and press.

6. Repeat this process to make a total of 16 geese each measuring 2¾" × 5" (7cm × 12.7cm) .

Make Each Placemat

Each placemat is made up of 4 panels and the pieced geese panel. Refer to the Layout Diagram as you assemble the placemats.

1. Construct the geese panel first. Sew 4 geese units along the long sides using a ¼" (6mm) seam. The points should all be facing the same way.

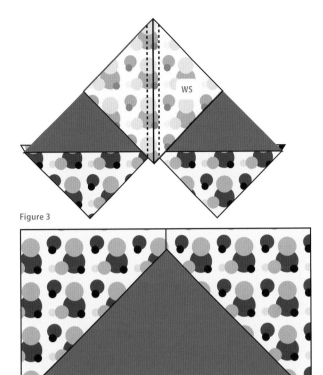

Figure 3

Figure 4

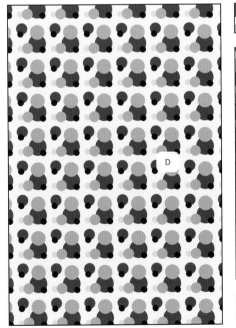

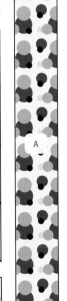

Layout Diagram

2. Sew Panel B and Panel C to the top and bottom of the geese panel.

3. Sew Panel A to the right side of the geese/B/C panel.

4. Sew Panel D to the left side of the geese/B/C panel.

5. Press the seams open. Repeat to piece 3 more placemats.

6. Layer each placemat with backing and batting. Baste and quilt.

7. Finish by binding with the remaining background fabric, in 2½" (6.4cm) wide strips.

CRAZY QUILT
Meshugana

by Andie

Crazy blocks are some of my favorite blocks to make. This method is very similar to the log cabin method, in that you build around a center piece toward the outside edges. It's a great way to use scraps, and they piece together very quickly. I like that every block is different using this fly-by-the-seat-of-your-pants method.

For this quilt, I used all creamy tones and neutrals, but in yummy textures to create variation within the tones. Crazy quilts are traditionally very ornate, but I wanted something clean and slightly masculine for this one. I used a neutral print for the middle piece in each block, which creates a little bit of additional interest.

FINISHED SIZE:	60" × 60"
	(152.4cm × 152.4cm)
LEVEL:	Beginner
QUILTED BY:	Jill Montgomery

Materials

½ to ¾ yard (.5m to .7m) each of 10–12 assorted cream/khaki fabrics (linen, cotton velveteen, heavy muslin, etc.)

25 scraps of neutral prints for middle pieces, each measuring at least 3" × 3" (7.6cm × 7.6cm)

3¼ yards (3m) of lightweight muslin

4 yards (3.7m) of standard-width fabric or 2 yards (1.8m) of 90" (35.4cm) wide fabric (backing)

½ yard (.5m) of coordinating fabric (binding)

Batting

Thread

Other

Basic quilting/sewing tools

Cutting

From the muslin, cut (25) 13" × 13" (33cm × 33cm) squares

Figure 1

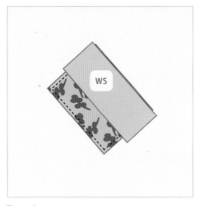

Figure 2

Figure 3

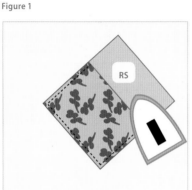

Figure 4

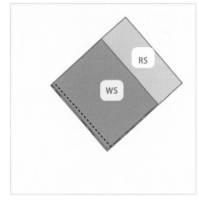

Figure 5A

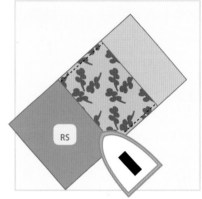

Figure 5B

Make the Blocks

1. Start with a middle printed piece. This can be any size or shape (as long as each edge is straight) and can be placed at any angle you like on top of the 13" (33cm) foundational square. With the right side of the fabric facing up, sew around the piece with a scant ¼" (6mm) allowance (Figure 1).

2. Add the next piece. This piece should line up along one edge of the starting piece. The raw edges of the new piece must be at least as long as the edge of the previous piece, but the width can be as wide as you like (Figure 2). The goal of every seam is to cover the previous

seam and build from the center out. It may take a few tries to get this technique just right, but it's fairly easy to get the hang of.

3. With right sides together, sew the second piece to the first using a ¼" (6mm) seam allowance (Figure 3).

4. Flip the second piece over so the right side is facing out and press flat (Figure 4).

5. Add the next piece. It can be placed on any side you choose. Again, place raw edges together, sew, flip over and press flat (Figures 5A and 5B).

6. Keep working your way around, adding fabric, until you've covered the entire muslin square (Figure 6). Vary your shapes and fabric to create interest and movement. Use diagonals, straight edges, asymmetry and composition to create direction. Sometimes you'll want to make a large piece of fabric from two or three smaller pieces of fabric to cover a large area. Sew the pieces together, press seams open and use as you would a single piece of fabric. Using this technique allows you to use smaller pieces that otherwise might be wasted.

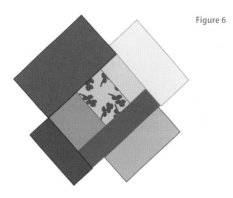

Figure 6

7. Square the block down to 12½" × 12½" (31.8cm × 31.8cm).

8. Edgestitch around the perimeter of the block using a basting stitch. This should be done with the back of block facing up (Figure 7).

Figure 7

9. Make 25 crazy blocks in this way.

Andie says…

Traditional crazy quilts are historically embellished heavily with decorative stitches. I love the idea of this, but I have little patience for hand quilting or stitching, so I let my machine do the work for me. Any decorative stitching should be done before piecing the quilt blocks together.

Assemble and Finish the Quilt

1. Using the Layout Diagram as a reference, arrange the blocks into 5 rows with 5 blocks in each row.

2. Sew the blocks together in rows, and then sew the rows together to complete the quilt top.

3. Layer the quilt top with backing and batting, then baste and quilt. This quilt was quilted very simply with a meander pattern to break up all the straight lines.

4. Finish by binding with 2¼" (5.7cm) wide coordinating fabric strips.

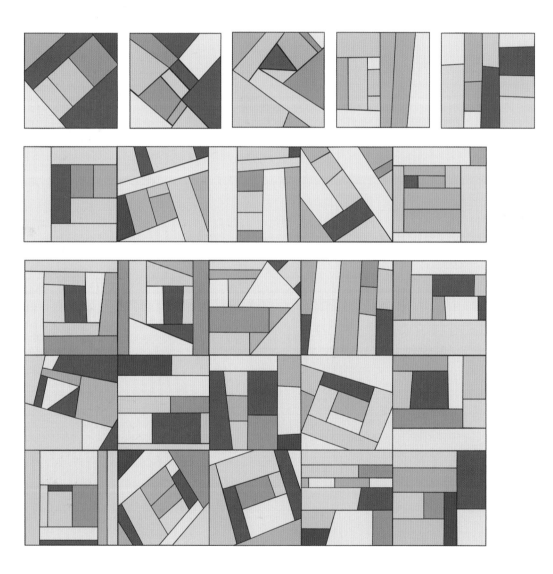

Layout Diagram

MESHUGANA QUILT

COINS QUILT
Pantone Pocket Change

by Kelly

I've loved rainbows ever since the days of scratch-and-sniff sticker collections. This modern interpretation of a coin quilt lets me bring rainbows back into my life in a more grownup way. You know, with fewer unicorns…

FINISHED SIZE:	72³/₄" × 88¹/₂"
	(184.8cm × 224.8cm)
LEVEL:	Beginner

Materials
(44) 2½" (6.4cm) wide jelly roll strips* (coins)

3½ yards (3.2m) of fabric (background, binding)

5¼ yards (4.8m) of standard-width fabric or 2¾ yards (2.5m) of 90" (228.6cm) wide fabric (backing)

Batting

Thread

Other
Basic quilting/sewing tools

* You may need more than one jelly roll to get a total of 44 strips, depending on the fabric manufacturer. I used the Dusty Kona Rollup by Robert Kaufman (see Resources on page 125).

6½" or 7"
(16.5cm or 17.8cm)

1¼"
(3.2cm)

Figure 1

Make the Quilt

1. Press each jelly roll strip. Lay out the jelly roll strips in order from top to bottom to create the desired effect.

Note: I placed my strips in rainbow order so the colors gradually gradate from one to the next, but you can lay yours out any way you like.

2. Measure the length of one jelly roll strip, and subcut each strip as indicated below (Figure 1). After you cut each strip, put it back in the order you determined in step 1. At the end of this, you will have 7 columns (1 skinny), each with fabrics arranged in the same way.

- **If the jelly rolls are 44" (111.8cm) long**, subcut each jelly roll strip into (6) 7" (17.8cm) sections and (1) 1¼" (3.2cm) section.
- **If the jelly rolls are 41"–43" (104.1cm–109.2cm) long**, subcut each jelly roll strip into (6) 6½" (16.5cm) sections and (1) 1¼" (3.2cm) section.

3. Using a ¼" (6mm) seam, sew the jelly roll sections together to create 6 identical coin columns and 1 skinny coin column, each column 44 jelly roll sections long (Figure 2). Press the seams in one direction.

¼"
(6mm)

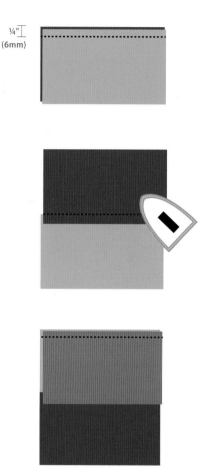

Figure 2

Kelly says…

I designed this quilt specifically to use these beautiful solid fabrics, but this quilt would be just as cool with prints. If you can't find a jelly roll that you like, or if you're a few jelly roll strips short of 44, don't despair. Jelly roll strips measure 2½" × WOF (6.4cm × WOF)— just cut your own!

4. From the background fabric, cut the following:

(5) 7½" × WOF strips (19.1cm × WOF)

(10) 4" × WOF strips (10.2cm × WOF)

(5) 3" × WOF strips (7.6cm × WOF)

5. Piece the strips from step 4 to make the following:

(2) 7½" × 88½" strips (19.1cm × 224.8cm)

(4) 4" × 88½" strips (10.2cm × 224.8cm)

(2) 3" × 88½" strips (7.6cm × 224.8cm)

6. Referring to the Layout Diagram, sew the background strips to the coin columns, being sure to rotate the second and sixth columns 180 degrees. Continue sewing the background strips and columns together until the entire quilt top is assembled. Press the seams toward the background fabric.

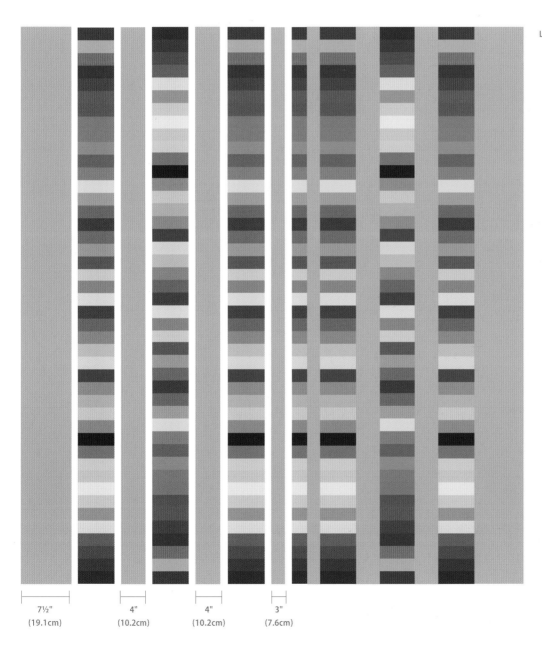

Layout Diagram

7½"	4"	4"	3"
(19.1cm)	(10.2cm)	(10.2cm)	(7.6cm)

7. Layer the quilt top with backing and batting, then baste and quilt. I quilted this top with a spiraling swirl in gray thread to help break up the linear design and add some movement.

8. Finish by binding with 2¼" (5.7cm) wide background fabric strips.

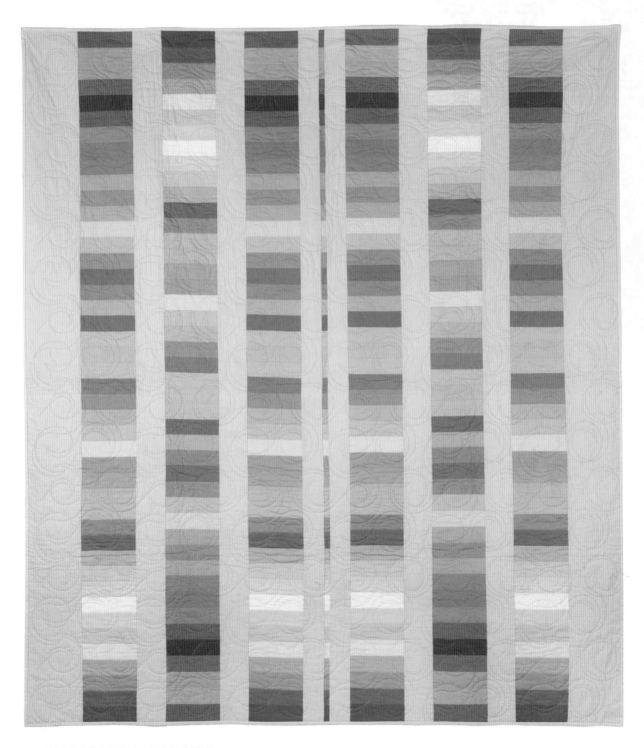

PANTONE POCKET CHANGE QUILT

POSTAGE STAMP QUILT
Snail Mail

by Kelly

Some days you don't want to cut around intricate templates, or pin curves, or fuss over the perfect background fabric choice. On those days, pull out these itty-bitty squares, plop down in front of your machine and just sew. It's not fast, but the slow simplicity is rewarding.

FINISHED SIZE:	56½" × 64½"
	(143.5cm × 163.8cm)
LEVEL:	Beginner

Materials

15 coordinating fat quarters (postage stamps)

1 yard (.9m) of an accent color fabric (inside border, binding)

3½" yards (3.2m) of standard-width fabric, 1¾ yards (1.6m) of 90" (228.6cm) wide fabric (backing)

Batting

Thread

Other

Box or bag for storing small fabric squares after cutting

Basic quilting/sewing tools

Make the Center Section

1. From 1 fat quarter, cut (8) 2½" (6.4cm) strips widthwise or parallel to the selvage. Without moving the strips, rotate the cutting mat 90 degrees and cut (7) 2½" (6.4cm) strips perpendicular to the first cuts, creating (56) 2½" (6.4cm) squares (Figure 1). I did not remove my selvages from the fabric for this quilt, but feel free to do so if you prefer (see page 56). Repeat to cut the remaining 14 fat quarters into 2½" (6.4cm) squares.

Note: You will need 788 squares for this quilt, and you will have extras after you finish cutting. Use them to piece the quilt backing or for a baby bib (see page 60).

2. As you cut the fabric squares, toss them into a large box. Once you have cut all your squares, place the box next to your sewing machine, and get ready to sew!

3. Randomly select two squares from the box. Place them right sides together and sew a ¼" (6mm) seam along one side (Figure 2). Continue sewing until you have sewn each square to another square. Don't press the seams. Place all of the sewn pairs back in the box.

4. Randomly select two pairs from the box. Place them right sides together and sew along one short side. Continue sewing until you have sewn each pair to another pair, creating strips of four squares. Don't press the seams. Place the strips back in the box.

5. Repeat this process, randomly selecting from the box each time. In this way, make:

- 28 rows of 24 squares each (don't press these seams yet)
- 2 rows of 26 squares each for top and bottom borders (press in one direction)
- 2 rows of 32 squares each for side borders (press in one direction)

6. Lay out the 28 rows of 24 squares. Move them around until you are happy with the placement (but don't agonize!). Very carefully, press all of the seams on the odd rows one direction, and all the seams on the even rows the other direction (Figure 3).

7. With right sides together, carefully pin and sew the rows together, nesting the seams together (see page 18) (Figure 4). Press the seam open. Repeat until the entire quilt top interior is sewn together.

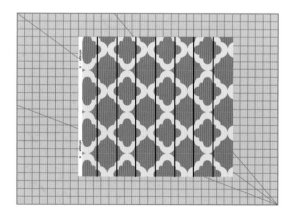

Figure 1

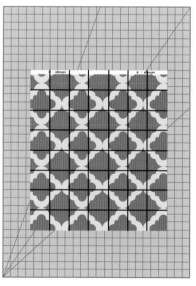

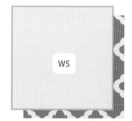

Figure 2

Make the Borders and Finish the Quilt

Refer to the Layout Diagram on page 56 as you complete the following steps.

1. From the accent fabric, cut (8) 2½" × WOF (6.4cm × WOF) strips.

2. Sew 2 accent strips together along one short end, and trim to 48½" (123.2cm) long. Sew this strip to the top edge of the quilt. Repeat to sew a second strip to the bottom edge of the quilt. Press the seams open.

3. Sew 2 accent strips together along one short end, and trim to 56½" (143.5cm) long. Sew this strip to one side of the quilt. Repeat to sew a second strip to the other side of the quilt. Press the seams open.

4. Place one of the rows of 26 squares right sides together with the top edge of the quilt. Pin carefully, making sure the postage stamp seams align with the edges of the accent borders. Sew the pieced row to the top edge of the quilt. Repeat to sew the other row of 26 squares to the bottom edge of the quilt. Press the seams open.

5. Sew one row of 32 squares to one side of the quilt, again carefully aligning the postage stamp seams with the edges of the accent borders. Repeat to sew the final row of 32 squares to the other side of the quilt. Press the seams open. This completes the quilt top.

6. Layer the quilt top with backing and batting, then baste and quilt. I used a tight meander (stipple) over the entire quilt (see page 56). This allowed me to thoroughly quilt over all of the seams and intersections, making the quilt more sturdy.

7. Finish by binding with 2¼" (5.7cm) wide accent fabric strips.

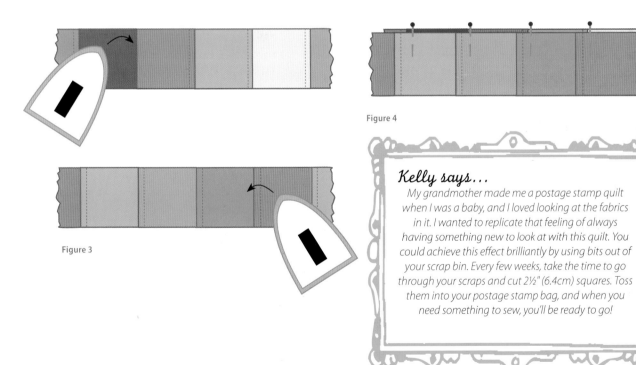

Figure 3

Figure 4

Kelly says…

My grandmother made me a postage stamp quilt when I was a baby, and I loved looking at the fabrics in it. I wanted to replicate that feeling of always having something new to look at with this quilt. You could achieve this effect brilliantly by using bits out of your scrap bin. Every few weeks, take the time to go through your scraps and cut 2½" (6.4cm) squares. Toss them into your postage stamp bag, and when you need something to sew, you'll be ready to go!

Layout Diagram

SALVAGE THE SELVAGES

I used the printed selvages in this quilt because they were as pretty as the fabric. If you decide to do this, please be sure to launder your quilt very carefully, as the selvages will shrink at a different rate than the rest of the fabric. If you have to wash the quilt, wash it on gentle and let it air dry.

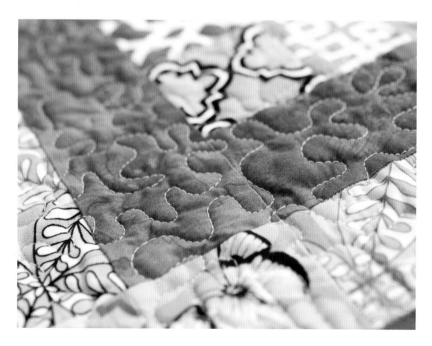

SNAIL MAIL QUILT

Baby Floor Quilt and Bib

by Kelly

This baby quilt is perfect for spreading on the floor for the itty-bitty to lounge around on, and a matching bib makes for a great gift package at a baby shower. Both are ideal for using a gorgeous hunk of fabric that you can't stand to cut up into little bits.

FINISHED SIZE:	30½" × 30½"
	(77.5cm × 77.5cm)
LEVEL:	Beginner
QUILTED BY:	Alice Biscopink

Materials

(for quilt)

¾ yard (.7m) of large print focus fabric (center square)

¼ yard (.2m) of complementary fabric (inside border)

Scraps and remnants of 6–12 coordinating prints; approximately ½ yard (.5m) total (postage stamps)

1 yard (.9m) of fabric (backing)

⅓ yard (.3m) of accent fabric (binding)

Batting

Thread

Other

Basic quilting/sewing tools

Cutting

From the large print focus fabric, fussy cut (1) 18½" (47cm) center square

From the complementary border fabric, cut:

- (2) 2½" × 18½" (6.4cm × 47cm) border strips
- (2) 2½" × 22½" (6.4cm × 57.2cm) border strips

From the assorted coordinating prints, cut (88) 2½" (6.4cm) squares

From the large print focus fabric, fussy cut (4) 4½" (11.4cm) squares

Make the Quilt

1. Sew the short border strips to the top and bottom of the center square (Figure 1). Press the strips out.

2. Sew the long border strips to the right and left side of the center square. Press the strips out.

3. Lay out (22) 2½" (6.4cm) squares into 2 rows of 11 squares each. Don't fuss with the arrangement too much—just make sure that two identical fabrics are not directly next to one another. Sew each row of squares together. Press the seams of one row to the right, and the seams of the other row to the left. Pin and sew the two rows together, carefully nesting the seams (Figure 2). Repeat to make three more panels like this.

4. Sew a pieced panel from the previous step to the top and bottom of the quilt, carefully aligning interior seams in the panel with the inner border seam (see the Layout Diagram on page 60).

5. Sew one of the 4½" (11.4cm) fussy-cut squares to each end of the two remaining pieced panels (see the Layout Diagram). These panels will be sewn to the sides of the center square; keep this in mind if the fussy-cut 4½" (11.4cm) squares have a print direction.

Figure 2

Kelly says…
Fussy cutting means that when you cut a shape from your fabric, you do so with a specific part of the fabric in mind. In other words, you cut out a specific image from the printed fabric, rather than randomly cutting the shape you need.

Figure 1

59

6. Sew a pieced panel from the previous step to each side of the quilt top, carefully aligning the interior seams in the panel with the interior seams of the rest of the quilt.

7. Layer, baste and quilt, using a dense stitch for durability.

8. Finish by binding with 2¼" (5.7cm) wide accent fabric strips.

Layout Diagram

Materials
(for bib)

Scrap of large print focus fabric

Scrap of complementary border fabric

Scraps of 6–12 coordinating prints

Batting: 10" × 11" (25.4cm × 27.9cm)

Backing: 10" × 11" (25.4cm × 27.9cm)

1 yard (.9m) of ¼" (6mm) wide ribbon

Other

Bib template (page 123)

Fine-tipped fabric pen

Basic quilting/sewing tools

Make It

1. From the assorted coordinating prints, cut (12) 2½" (6.4cm) squares. From the large print focus fabric, fussy cut a 2½" × 8½" (6.4cm × 21.6cm) rectangle.

Note: If your focus fabric print is too wide to fussy cut down to a 2½" (6.4cm) wide strip, cut out a 4½" × 8½" (11.4cm × 21.6cm) strip instead, and eliminate (4) 2½" (6.4cm) squares.

2. Lay out the 12 small squares into 3 columns of 4 squares each, with the fussy-cut rectangle in between two of the columns. Make sure that two identical fabrics are not directly next one another. Sew the squares together into 3 columns, and then sew the columns (including the fussy-cut rectangle) together. Carefully match and pin intersecting seams. Use the final project image as a reference. Press open.

3. From the complementary border fabric, cut (1) 2½" × 8½" (6.4cm × 21.6cm) strip (top) and two 2½" × 12½" (6.4cm × 21.6cm) strips (sides). Sew the short strip to the top of the pieced rectangle. Press open. Sew a long strip to each side of the pieced rectangle. Press open.

4. Enlarge and cut out the bib template. Fold the template vertically in half to find the center. Open it and place the template on top of the pieced rectangle. Align the center fold with the center seam. Align the template vertically until you're satisfied with the placement, but make sure there is fabric under the entire template. Use a fine-tipped fabric pen to trace around the edges of the template onto the fabric.

5. Cut out the bib shape from the pieced rectangle. Cut out one bib template shape from the backing and one from the batting.

6. Cut the ribbon in half to make (2) 18" (45.7cm) long pieces. Sew one end of each ribbon to the top corner of the wrong side of the bib; stitch approximately ⅛" (3mm) from the edge of the bib so the stitches are hidden in a later seam allowance. Backstitch several times.

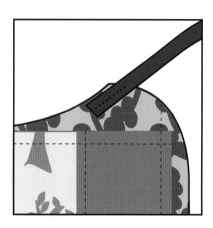

Figure 1

7. Place the bib top and back right sides together, with the batting in the middle. Pin around the edges, and tuck the ribbon inside the sandwich. Stitch a ¼" (6mm) seam around the entire bib edge, leaving a 3" (7.6cm) hole along the bottom edge for turning.

8. Turn the bib right side out. Press under the turning hole edges and pin in place. Edgestitch around the entire bib perimeter, strengthening the edges and closing the turning hole.

9. Quilt the bib as normal, and you're all set to give it to your favorite dribble monster!

Note: I tied a knot in each end of the ribbon to secure it from fraying all the way; you can also turn the ribbon ends under and stitch to secure.

Spider Web Quilt
Effie's Web
by Andie

What a hoot this quilt is! So much color, so much movement. The technique for this block is based on a string quilt. String quilts are a fantastic way to use up scraps. It's also a technique that is favored by modern quilters, as it lends itself well to the improvisational style. You can make this block very precise and structured, or make it with asymmetry and freedom. Either way, it's super fun.

FINISHED SIZE:	55" × 55"
	(139.7cm × 139.7cm)
LEVEL:	Intermediate
QUILTED BY:	Jenny Pedigo

Materials

16 fat quarters

2½–3 yards (2.3m to 2.7m) of assorted scraps* for the strings, each at least 1" (2.5cm) wide and up to 8" (20.3cm) long

¾ yard (.7m) of fabric (border)

½ yard (.5m) of fabric (binding)

3½ yards (3.2m) of standard-width fabric or 1¾ yards (1.6m) of 90" (228.6cm) wide fabric (backing)

Batting

Thread

* I used all juicy, bright colors for this quilt. Using similar tones and themes will give a more cohesive feel to the finished quilt. Some of the leftover fat quarters and border fabric can be used in the strings for the webs.

Other

Template (page 123)

Template plastic

Pencil or tailor's chalk

Basic quilting/sewing tools

Cutting

1. From each fat quarter, cut one 12½" (31.8cm) square. Cut each square in half diagonally. Cut on the diagonal again, creating 4 triangles (64 total) (Figure 1).

2. From the scraps, cut strips of fabric from 1"–3" (2.5cm to 7.6cm) wide and 2"–8" (5.1cm to 20.3cm) long. As you cut, separate the strips into piles of similar colors. This will make it easier to create variation when piecing the blocks later.

3. From the border fabric, cut (9) 12½" (31.8cm) squares. Cut each square in half diagonally. Cut on the diagonal again, creating 4 triangles (36 total).

Make the Block

1. Using the template, trace the pattern onto the right side of each large triangle using a pencil or tailor's chalk. This will be the guideline for sewing the first string, so make the line easy to see and follow.

2. Begin with a large triangle, long side toward you and the point facing away, right side facing up. Let's do the right side first: Place the first string piece, which should be at least 5" (12.7cm) long, right sides together with the triangle. The raw edge of the string piece should be lined up with the marked

template pattern line. Pin the strip in place to prevent shifting. Sew a ¼" (6mm) seam along the inside edge of the marked template line (Figure 2).

3. Flip the string piece open and press flat.

4. After the first string piece is sewn, fold under the large triangle corner toward the middle. From this point on, you will be attaching the rest of the strings to the first attached string, not the base triangle (Figure 3).

5. Keep sewing strips to each other, using a ¼" (6mm) seam allowance (Figure 4).

6. Flip the base triangle back over. Make sure your pieced strings cover the triangle corner. Add another strip to the end if the set is too short.

7. Repeat with the other side of triangle (Figure 5).

8. After both sides of the triangle have been pieced, flip the triangle over. On a cutting mat, use a rotary cutter and a straightedge to trim the strings even with the edges of the original base triangles (Figure 6).

9. Flip the trimmed triangle over so the right side is facing up. Fold each string-pieced side back and trim the background fabric ¼" (6mm) away from the first seam on both sides. Add strings to the fat-quarter triangles and the border triangles in this way.

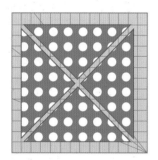

Figure 1

Figure 3

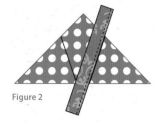

Figure 2

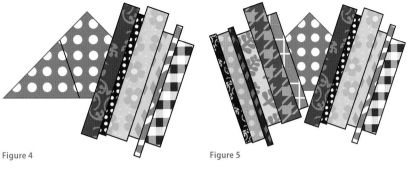

Figure 4

Figure 5

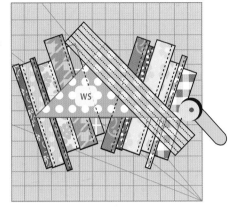

Figure 6

Middle Blocks

1. Sew together 4 triangles with matching backgrounds to make a middle block, so that the backgrounds form a star shape in the middle (Figure 7).

2. Trim each block to 11¼" (28.6cm). Make 16 blocks in this way from the 16 fat-quarter backgrounds.

Border Blocks

1. Follow the same steps you did for the middle blocks and piece the border fabric triangles into blocks.

2. Trim each block to 11¼" (28.6cm). Make 9 border blocks in this way (Figure 8).

3. Cut 8 of the border blocks in half (Figure 9). Cut the remaining block into quarters for the corners (Figure 10). You will end up with 16 border rectangles and 4 border squares.

Figure 7

Figure 8

Figure 9

Figure 10

Finish the Quilt

1. Using the Layout Diagram as a reference, sew the middle blocks into 4 rows of 4 blocks each.

2. Sew together 4 rows of 4 border rectangles each, end to end, watching the block orientation. Sew 1 border square to each end of 2 of these rows. The web portion of the square should be facing inward, with the border print facing out to the corner.

3. Sew the 2 short borders to the top and bottom of the quilt. Then sew the 2 long borders to each side of the quilt.

4. Layer the quilt top with backing and batting, then baste and quilt. This quilt was quilted to emphasize the star design created by the background fabrics.

5. Finish by binding with 2¼" (5.7cm) wide coordinating fabric strips.

Layout Diagram

Andie says...

I originally made this quilt for an online challenge (which won Judge's Choice, thankyouverymuch). The idea was to swap "ugly" fabric with a partner and design a quilt using that fabric along with fabric from our stash. We were limited to purchasing only one cut of fabric. My swap partner, Sharon, was very kind to me and sent me great fabrics that she thought I would like. The rest of the fabrics came from my stash, and I purchased the blue floral that borders the outside of the quilt.

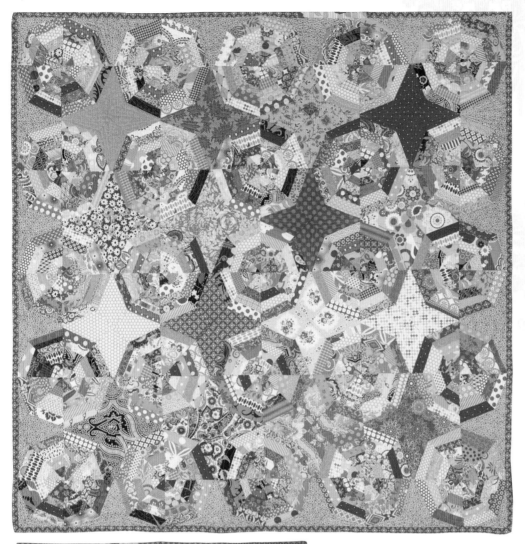

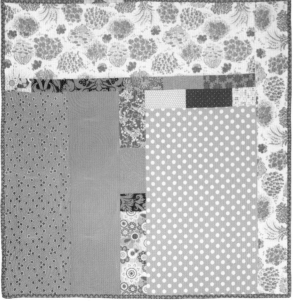

EFFIE'S WEB QUILT

I used only prints in this quilt. There's only one tiny piece of solid fabric in it! I also pieced the back (shown at left), which I love just as much as the front.

String-Pieced Tablerunner

by Andie

I absolutely love this kind of project! It combines some of my favorite things in a quilting project—unusual color pairings, improvisational piecing, contrived dishevelment—and it's super-fast to throw together. There's just something about the juxtaposition of a slightly haphazard interior inside a crisp, perfect frame. . .

FINISHED SIZE:	60" × 13"
	(152.4cm × 33cm)(sizes will vary)
LEVEL:	Beginner

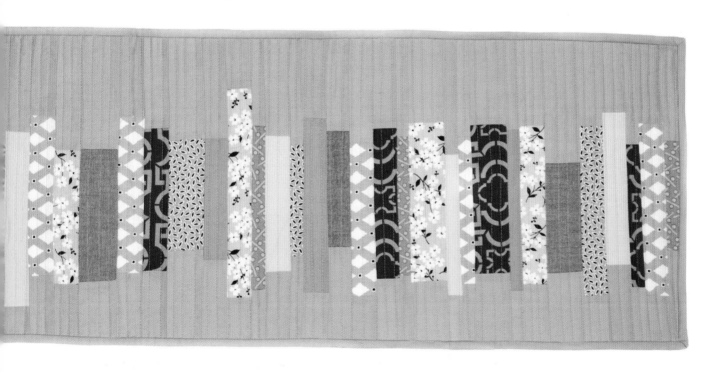

Materials

¾ yard (.7m) total of a variety of gray solids and prints (I used large scraps of 8 different fabrics)

2 yards (1.8m) of robin's egg blue fabric (background, binding)

1½ yards (1.4m) of fabric (backing)

Batting

Thread

Other

Basic quilting/sewing tools

Andie says...

A most decidedly modern aspect of this project is the reverse-neutral situation (I totally made up that term) set up by the fabric choices. Here we have gray acting as the focal color against a backdrop of robin's egg blue. What? A neutral as the focal color instead of a "real" color? Why not! And the use of different shades of gray with mixed prints creates depth and movement.

Make the Tablerunner

1. From the gray fabrics, cut strips that are 1" (2.5cm), 1½" (3.8cm) and 2" (5.1cm) wide and anywhere from 3½" to 5" (8.9cm to 12.7cm) long. Create a wide variety of widths versus lengths within your gray fabrics. You'll need 75–100 strips.

2. From the background fabric, cut strips that are 1" (2.5cm), 1½" (3.8cm) and 2" (5.1cm) wide and 6" (15.2cm) long. Cut double what you cut for the gray fabric.

3. Sew a background strip to each end of each gray strip, matching widths (Figure 1). Press open.

4. Separate the strips into piles of similar lengths. Begin sewing the strips together so the sections look as if they're being stacked, making sure to vary the gray fabrics and stagger the centers a little (Figure 2). Make each unit of stacked strips 10"–12" (25.4cm to 30.5cm) tall. This will be your block. Press all seams to one side.

5. Make 5 or 6 stacked blocks in this way, until you have used all your strips.

6. Sew the blocks end to end to create one long stack of strips.

Figure 1

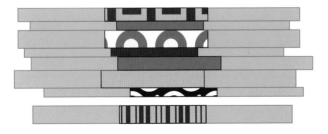

7. Layer the tablerunner with backing and batting, then baste and quilt. Trim the edges of the rectangle to square it up.

8. Finish by binding with 2¼" (5.7cm) wide coordinating fabric strips.

Figure 2

Les Elefants et Hippos

by Andie

I used to sing a song to my kids when they were little called "One Elephant." I first learned it when I was young and taking French classes. We sang songs "en français" to help us learn the language better, and this one stuck in my head. This quilt reminds me of that fun song, sung by my little ones in their sweet voices.

FINISHED SIZE:	40½" × 40½" (102.9cm × 102.9cm)
LEVEL:	Intermediate

Materials

1 yard (.9m) neutral graphic print fabric

4 fat quarters of Japanese novelty prints

2 yards (1.8m) fabric (backing)

⅜ yard (.4m) coordinating fabric (binding)

Batting

Thread

Other

Small cutting mat

Basic quilting/sewing tools

Cutting

From each fat quarter, cut (8) 6" (15.2cm) squares

From the neutral graphic fabric, cut (32) 6" (15.2cm) squares

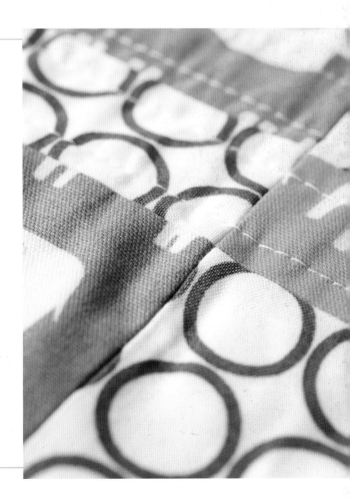

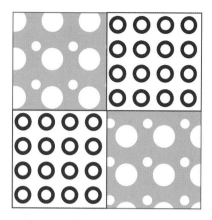

Figure 1

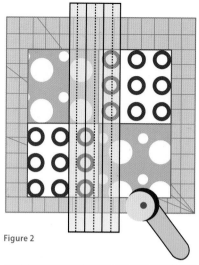

Figure 2

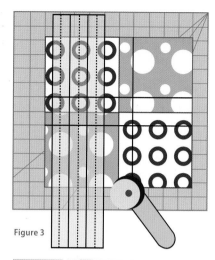

Figure 3

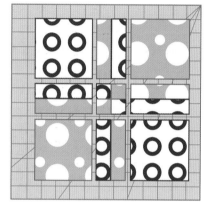

Figure 4

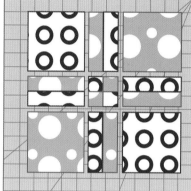

Figure 5

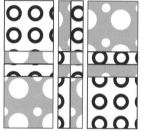

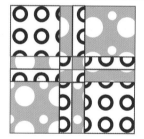

Figure 6

Make the Blocks

1. Sew 2 matching novelty print squares and 2 neutral graphic squares into a checkerboard 4-patch (Figure 1). Press well.

2. Place your 4-patch on a small cutting mat so that you can turn the mat (and not the block) as you make the following cuts:

- Cut 1½" (3.8cm) to either side of the center seam (Figure 2). Don't move the fabric after each cut; leave it in the same position.
- Rotate the cutting mat 90 degrees, and cut 1½" (3.8cm) to either side of the center seam (Figure 3).

3. Now you will swap pieces. First, switch the top and bottom center pieces so that the bottom piece is on the top and the top piece is on the bottom. Don't rotate the pieces; just switch places (Figure 4).

4. Do the same with the left and right center pieces (Figure 5).

5. Sew the 9 sections together to form 3 columns.

6. Sew the 3 columns together. Square the block to 10½" × 10½" (26.7cm × 26.7cm) to finish the block (Figure 6).

7. Make a total of 16 blocks in this way (4 from each fat quarter).

Andie says...

This quilt is made from heavier Japanese fabric, which makes it a little easier to cut, sew and hold up through laundering and serious snuggling. It comes in bold and juicy colors, quirky and fun graphic prints, and is most often available in linen/cotton blends. It's more expensive than the average fabric, but well worth the price for a unique and funky quilt.

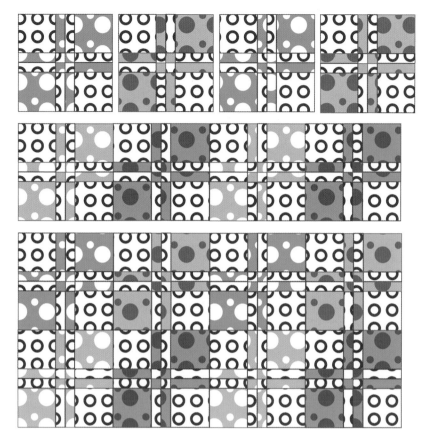

Layout Diagram

Assemble and Finish the Quilt

1. Using the Layout Diagram as a reference, arrange the blocks into 4 rows, with 4 blocks in each row. Alternate the blocks so identical blocks don't wind up next to each other.

2. Sew the blocks together in rows, and then sew the rows together to complete the quilt top.

3. Layer the quilt top with backing and batting, then baste and quilt. This quilt was quilted very simply with straight line stitching, since the fabrics were already so wild!

4. Finish by binding with 2¼" (5.7cm) wide coordinating fabric strips.

Andie says…

I actually made one of these blocks wrong. I could tell you it was intentional, but it wasn't. This gives me an opportunity to point out that even though I made a mistake, the quilt still turned out great. Some believe that the Amish make every quilt with an intentional mistake to remind the quilt maker and the recipient that humans are flawed and imperfect, and that only God is perfect. Intentional or not, mistakes can be considered a sweet and endearing addition to a quilt.

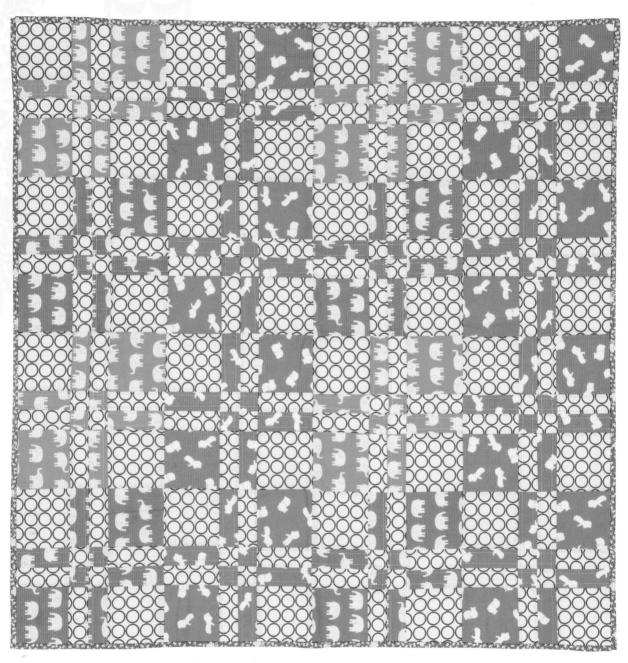

LES ELEFANTS ET HIPPOS QUILT

La Femme de la Mer Quilt

by Kelly

Mermaids and giant squids, sea nymphs and turtles, orange and pink, stripes and ruffles… just a few of my favorite things, all rolled into one.

FINISHED SIZE:	34½" × 44½" (87.6cm × 113cm)
LEVEL:	Intermediate

Materials

½ yard (.5m) of main print A fabric

½ yard (.5m) of main print B fabric

¼ yard (.2m) of solid color A fabric

¼ yard (.2m) of solid color B fabric

2 yards (1.8m) of coordinating striped fabric

Backing: 2 yards (1.8m) of fabric (backing)

2 yards (1.8m) coordinating fabric (ruffled binding)

Batting

Thread

1 skein of coordinating embroidery floss

Other

Heavy tapestry needle

Basic quilting/sewing tools

Cutting

From main print A fabric, cut (12) 6" (15.2cm) squares

From main print B fabric, cut (12) 6" (15.2cm) squares

From solid color A fabric, cut (6) 6" (15.2cm) squares

From solid color B fabric, cut (6) 6" (15.2cm) squares

From striped fabric, cut (12) 6" (15.2cm) squares

From ruffled binding fabric, cut (12) 5" × WOF
(12.7cm × WOF) strips

From backing fabric and batting, cut a 34½" × 44½"
(87.6cm × 113cm) rectangle

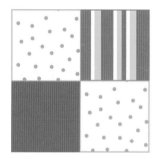

Figure 1

Figure 2

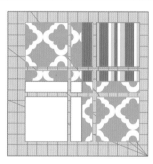

Figure 3

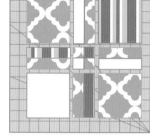

Figure 4

Make and Assemble the Quilt

1. Sew 2 main print A squares, 1 solid A square and 1 striped square into a checkerboard 4-patch, with the main print squares in diagonal corners (Figure 1). Repeat to make 6 total 4-patches like this.

2. Sew 2 main print B squares, 1 solid B square and 1 striped square into a checkerboard 4-patch, with the main print squares in diagonal corners (Figure 2). Repeat to make 6 total 4-patches like this.

3. Referring to steps 2–6 on page 72, cut each block into nine pieces, swap the center sections, sew the block back together and square to 10½" × 10½" (26.7cm × 26.7cm) (Figures 3 and 4).

4. Arrange the blocks into 4 rows with 3 blocks in each row. Alternate the blocks so identical blocks don't wind up next to each other.

5. Sew the blocks together in rows, and then sew the rows together to complete the quilt top.

6. Using the technique on page 17 for cutting on the bias, cut at least 170" (431.8cm) of 2½" (6.4cm) wide bias-cut strips from the remaining striped fabric. Join the strips end to end with diagonal seams (as you would to make binding) to make borders the following lengths (Figure 5):

- (2) 2½" × 34½" (6.4cm × 87.6cm) strips (top and bottom borders)
- (2) 2½" × 40½" (6.4cm × 102.9cm) strips (side borders)

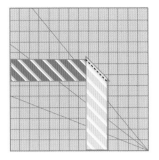

Figure 5

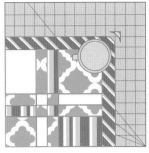

Figure 6

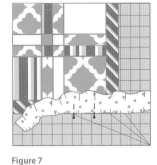

Figure 7

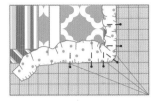

Figure 8

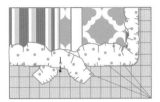

Figure 9

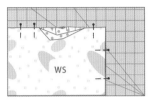

Figure 10

Figure 11

7. Sew the 2 longer strips to either side of the quilt. Then sew the 2 shorter strips to the top and bottom of the quilt.

8. Sew the 12 ruffled binding strips end to end to make one long strip. Press the strip in half lengthwise with wrong sides together.

9. Referring to the technique for making ruffles on pages 28–29, ruffle the entire long strip of fabric on the tightest ruffle setting your foot has (on most, a "1"). Be sure that as you sew, the ruffler is stitching along the two raw edges.

10. Use a coffee mug to trace and cut round corners on your quilt (Figure 6).

11. Starting at one end of the ruffles, place the ruffles along the edge of the quilt, aligning the raw edges. Let the end you start with hang off the edge of the quilt (Figure 7).

12. Pin the ruffles in place all the way around the quilt, gently easing around the corners (Figure 8).

13. When you get back to where you started, cross the end of the ruffle strip across the first end and down off the edge (Figure 9). Play with how you cross the ends so there isn't a gap between the two ends.

14. Using a ⅛" (3.2mm) seam allowance, sew around the perimeter of the quilt to attach the ruffles to the edge.

15. Trim the overhanging ruffle ends even with the quilt edge.

16. Place the quilt top right side up on top of the batting. The ruffles should be flopped over onto the quilt top. Place the backing fabric right side down on top of the quilt top and batting, sandwiching the ruffles inside (Figure 10). Carefully pin all the layers together around the perimeter of the quilt.

17. Using a ¼" (6mm) seam allowance, sew around the perimeter of the quilt. Leave an 8"–10" (20.3cm to 25.4cm) opening in this seam.

18. Turn the quilt through the opening, and then stitch it closed by hand.

19. Using the technique on page 30, tie your quilt using coordinating embroidery floss and a heavy-duty tapestry needle (Figure 11).

Urban Cabin

by Kelly

My apartment, though it's small, is one of my favorite places because it's all mine——a little haven to shut out the crazy world outside. This quilt is a marriage of my two personalities: the city girl who loves falling asleep to the sound of traffic at night, and the one who loves the cozy quiet of a winter night, curled up in a quilt.

FINISHED SIZE:	56" × 93"
	(142.2cm × 236.2cm)
LEVEL:	Intermediate
QUILTED BY:	Jill Montgomery

Materials

1¾ yards (1.6m) gray solid fabric

1¾ yards (1.6m) white solid fabric

⅓ yard (.3m) focus print (block centers)

16 coordinating print fat quarters

¾ yard (.7m) coordinating fabric (binding)

Batting

Thread

Note on backing: This odd-sized quilt is tricky to back. I suggest piecing a back with scraps like I did (see photo on page 84), or using extra-wide fabric specifically for quilt backing. If using standard-width backing, you'll need 5⅜" (136cm). If you use wide fabric (usually around 90" [228.6cm] wide), you will need 2¾ yards (2.5m) to back this quilt.

Other

Basic quilting/sewing tools

Quilter's spray starch (optional; see Resources on page 125)

Cutting

From the focus print fabric, cut (16) 4" (10.2cm) squares for the block centers

From the gray solid fabric, cut the following strips:

- (8) 2" × 4" (5.1cm × 10.2cm)
- (16) 2" × 7" (5.1cm × 17.8cm)
- (16) 2" × 10" (5.1cm × 25.4cm)
- (16) 2" × 13" (5.1cm × 33cm)
- (16) 2" × 16" (5.1cm × 40.6cm)
- (8) 2" × 19" (5.1cm × 48.3cm)

From the white solid fabric, cut the following strips:

- (8) 2" × 4" (5.1cm × 10.2cm)
- (16) 2" × 7" (5.1cm × 17.8cm)
- (16) 2" × 10" (5.1cm × 25.4cm)
- (16) 2" × 13" (5.1cm × 33cm)
- (16) 2" × 16" (5.1cm × 40.6cm)
- (8) 2" × 19" (5.1cm × 48.3cm)

From each of the 16 coordinating fat quarters, cut the following strips:

- (2) 2" × 5½" (5.1cm × 14cm)
- (2) 2" x 8½" (5.1cm × 21.6cm)
- (2) 2" × 11½" (5.1cm × 29.2cm)
- (2) 2" × 14½" (5.1cm × 36.8cm)
- (2) 2" × 17½" (5.1cm × 44.5cm)

Sort and Shuffle Your Fabric Strips

1. Press all of your fabric strips extremely well. I recommend using quilter's spray starch (see Resources on page 125).

2. Sort your printed coordinating fabric strips into piles according to size, placing the fabrics in the same order in each pile. Line up the piles from left to right, from shortest to longest. There will be 10 piles with 16 strips in each pile (Figure 1).

3. Moving from left to right, begin with the second pile of fabric. From the second pile, take 1 fabric strip off the top and move it to the bottom of the pile. From the third pile, take 2 strips off the top and move them to the bottom of the pile. From the fourth pile, move 3 strips to the bottom of the pile, and so forth, until you have done this to all 10 piles (Figure 2). This ensures that each block will be slightly different, and that no single fabric will be repeated in that block.

Sew the "A" Blocks

The A blocks will always begin with a gray strip next to the center square.

1. Sewing one block at a time, begin with a 4" (10.2cm) center square. Using a ¼" (6mm) seam, sew a 4" (10.2cm) gray strip along the top of the block. Press the strip open (Figure 3).

2. Moving in a clockwise direction, sew a 5½" (14cm) print strip (the top strip in your first pile) to the right side of the unit from step 1. Press the strip open (Figure 4).

3. Sew a 5½" (14cm) print strip (the top strip in your second pile) to the bottom side of the unit from the previous step. Press the strip open (Figure 5).

Figure 1

Figure 3

Figure 2

Figure 4

Figure 5

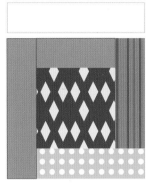

Figure 6   Figure 7   Figure 8

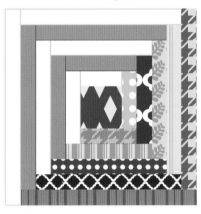

Figure 9 (Block A)   Figure 10 (Block B)

4. Sew a 7" (17.8cm) gray strip to the left side of the unit. Press the strip open (Figure 6).

5. Sew a 7" (17.8cm) white strip to the top of the unit. Press the strip open (Figure 7).

6. Continue adding strips, moving clockwise around the unit, rotating gray and white strips in each round, and always working in order from the top of the printed fabric piles. Add 5 full rounds of strips to complete the block (Figure 8).

7. Repeat steps 1–6 to make a total of 8 "A" blocks. Square each block to 19" × 19" (48.3cm × 48.3cm) (Figure 9).

Sew the "B" Blocks

The B blocks will always begin with a white strip next to the center square.

1. Sewing one block at a time, begin with a 4" (10.2cm) center square. Using a ¼" (6mm) seam, sew a 4" (10.2cm) white strip along the top of the block. Press the strip open.

2. Continue adding strips in the way described for the A block, being sure to always start with the white round closest to the center square. Add 5 full rounds of strips to complete the block.

3. Repeat to make a total of 8 "B" blocks. Square each block to 19" × 19" (48.3cm × 48.3cm) (Figure 10).

Kelly says…
Log cabins aren't difficult, they're just fussy. All that's required to make this quilt turn out beautifully is to really take your time on the basics: accurate cutting, careful pressing, meticulous ¼" (6mm) seams.

81

Assemble and Finish the Quilt

1. Using the Layout Diagram as a reference, arrange the blocks into 5 rows with 3 blocks in each row, alternating A and B blocks. Rotate the blocks so the white/gray section forms diagonal rows, and the colorful section forms diagonal rows. You will have 1 block left over.

2. Sew the blocks together into rows, and then sew the rows together to complete the quilt top.

3. Layer the quilt top with backing and batting, then baste and quilt. This quilt was quilted with concentric diamonds in each block to add some additional movement to the quilt, but still keep the design very geometric.

4. Finish by binding with 2¼" (5.7cm) wide coordinating fabric strips.

Note: I used scraps from my fat quarters to piece a binding, which you can certainly do if you have extras from your fat quarters. You will need approximately 310" (7.9m) of binding for this quilt.

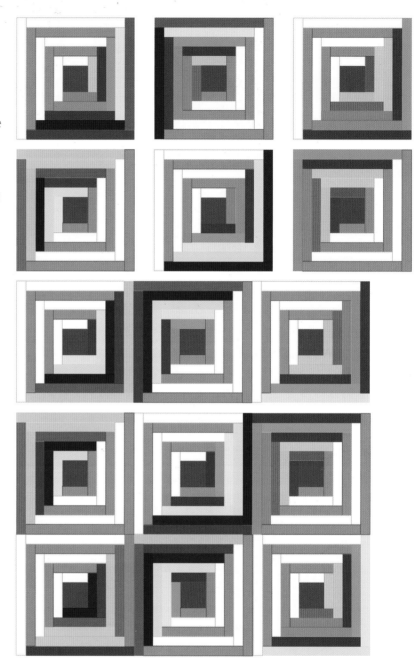

Layout Diagram

URBAN CABIN QUILT

URBAN CABIN (BACK)

The focus fabric used as the center of each log cabin block was my inspiration for choosing the rest of the fabrics. I found a beautiful piece of fabric with great colors, and chose 16 fabrics that coordinated with it. I then used a large piece of that focus fabric on the back (shown below) so everyone can see where my inspiration came from!

Kelly says...

You made 16 blocks for this quilt, but you only need 15. So what do you do with that extra block? With 16 blocks, you have an "alternate" in case you don't like how one of the blocks is playing with the others—just swap 'em out! An extra block is also great to piece into the back of the quilt, or to make a fast and easy coordinating throw pillow. In the case of this quilt, it also gives you an alternate layout possibility: arrange your blocks in 4 rows of 4 blocks to make a square quilt.

MINI-PROJECT
Wall Art
by Kelly

Fabric is art all by itself (especially when you find great
pictorial fabrics like The Ghastlies from Alexander Henry).
A little piecing, some top stitching and a blank canvas allow
you to turn the fabric you love into wall art for your home.

FINISHED SIZE:	Will vary
LEVEL:	Easy

Materials

Canvas stretched on a frame (any desired size)

Focus fabric piece (see Resources on page 125)

Coordinating scraps (logs)

Small scrap of white fabric (for name plaque)

Double-sided fusible web (scrap)

Coordinating/contrasting thread

Name plaque template (page 122)

Other

Basic quilting/sewing tools

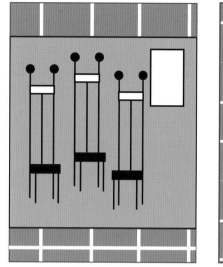

Figure 1

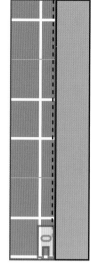

Figure 2

Kelly says...

Thumbtacks are temporary and easily removable, so make a bunch of these fabric pieces and swap them out when you get sick of looking at one!

Make the Art Piece

1. Fussy cut a square or rectangular section from your focus fabric to be the center of your art piece. It can be any size, but the larger it is (in comparison to your canvas), the less room you will have to add extra fabric. I recommend cutting a center section about half as big both horizontally and vertically as your canvas.

2. Cut 1½" (2.5cm) wide strips from your coordinating fabrics.

3. Measure the width of your center piece. Sew a 1½" (2.5cm) strip this length to the top and bottom of your center piece. Press the strips open (Figure 1).

4. To add an additional decorative element, topstitch the pressed open strip about ⅛" (3mm) away from the seam using a coordinating/contrasting thread (Figure 2).

5. Trim the right and left edges of the center unit even. Measure the unit from top to bottom. Cut two 1½" (3.8cm) strips this length and sew them to either side of the center unit. Press open and topstitch.

Figure 3

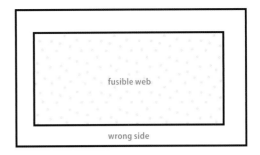

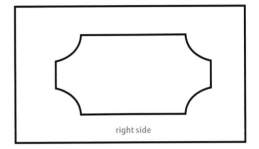

Figure 4

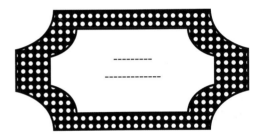

Figure 5

6. Continue measuring the center unit and adding 1½" (3.8cm) strips in this way (top and bottom, then sides), pressing open and topstitching each section as you go. Once you have pieced a unit that's almost the size of the top of your canvas, sew a final round using extra-wide strips (about 5" [12.7cm] wide rather than 1½" [3.8cm]) (Figure 3).

7. Fuse double-sided fusible web to the back of a small piece of white fabric. Cut the name plaque template out of the white fabric. Stitch (using freemotion sewing techniques) or write with permanent marker the name of your art piece onto the white plaque (Figure 4).

8. Fuse the white plaque to a larger contrasting fabric piece, and cut out a mirroring shape (Figure 5). Topstitch the plaque onto your fabric piece, just under the center focus fabric.

9. Measure to find and mark the center of your canvas. Measure and mark the center of your fabric piece. Using the two center marks to help you, carefully wrap the fabric around the canvas, making sure the piece is straight and centered.

10. Wrap and tuck the fabric around the corners of the canvas, like you would gift wrap a present. Use thumbtacks to secure the fabric to the back of the frame (Figure 6).

Figure 6

HEXAGON QUILT
Ali's Lullaby

by Andie

This quilt is all about color! Bright, bold color that's set against a stark white background is truly modern in every sense. The English paper-pieced hexagons were so much fun to make. I don't normally do a lot of hand sewing, but these little gems were a welcome project. They assemble so quickly and they're totally portable, which is a great way to fill the time in waiting rooms and while traveling.

FINISHED SIZE:	32½" × 34½"
	(82.6cm × 87.6cm)
LEVEL:	Intermediate

Materials

1 yard (.9m) of white solid (background)

¼ yard (.2m)* each of coral, aqua, plum and fuchsia prints (hexies, borders)

4 fat eighths each of coral, aqua, plum and fuchsia prints (hexies)

⅓ yard (.3m) of coordinating fabric (binding)

1 yard (.9cm) of fabric (backing)

Batting

Thread

* Do not use fat quarters for this cut; you need a WOF cut for the borders.

Other

Approximately 50 paper hexagon templates (page 122), measuring 2" (5.1cm) from point to point

Hand sewing needle

Coordinating threads in all 4 colors, or invisible thread

Basic quilting/sewing tools

Cutting

Cut (4) 3½" (8.9cm) strips from each color of the ¼ yard (.2m) fabrics (WOF)

Cut (4–6) 3" (7.6cm) squares from the leftover fabric and the fat eighths, creating a random number of each print (Total of 26 of each color.)

Cut one solid white piece 28½" × 26½" (72.4cm × 67.3cm)

Make and Finish the Quilt

1. Referring to the English paper-piecing technique on pages 24–25, make 26 hexies in all 4 colorways, using either invisible or coordinating thread.

Figure 1

2. Sew 26 hexies of 1 colorway together into a double-wide strip of 13 hexies on each side (Figure 1). Make 1 strip in each of the 4 colorways.

3. Position the hexie strips on the white background rectangle. Pin the outer strips (fuchsia and aqua) 3½" (8.9cm) from the longest side of the white background piece, and 2½" (6.4cm) from the shorter end of the white background piece.

4. Pin the middle hexie strips (coral and plum) so they are 2" (5.1cm) away from each other and 2" (5.1cm) away from the outer hexie strips. They will also be 2½" (6.4cm) from the shorter edge of the white background fabric. Line them up so they look even and centered.

5. Using a zigzag stitch and coordinating thread, appliqué the hexie strips onto the background fabric. You can also use a straight stitch for this if you like.

6. Referring to the Layout Diagram, sew the plum and coral strips to the top and bottom of the quilt. Trim the ends even with the sides of the quilt.

7. Sew the fuchsia and aqua strips to the sides of the quilt. Trim the ends even with the top and bottom of the quilt.

8. Square up the quilt. Layer the top with backing and batting (2 layers if desired), then baste and quilt.

9. Finish by binding with 2¼" (5.7cm) wide bright fabric strips.

Andie says…

Baby quilts usually fall into two categories: heirlooms and ones made for serious cuddling. I love to make baby quilts that will get used, so I tend to construct them in a more heavy-duty manner. I almost always bind them with my machine and I like to do heavy quilting. I also use two layers of batting to make them extra soft and cuddly.

2½" (6.4cm)   2" (5.1cm)

Layout Diagram

ALI'S LULLABY QUILT

Hexie Pillow
by Andie

Pillows are a fun and easy way to add your own handmade style into any décor. They're quick to put together and pretty inexpensive, especially when the ready-made pillow forms go on sale at the large chain fabric and craft stores. This hexie pillow is made to go in my living room, which my kids call "the talking room." It adds a huge punch of color and a bit of whimsy in an otherwise formal room.

FINISHED PILLOW SIZE:
20" square (50.1cm)
LEVEL: Intermediate

Materials

22" (55.9cm) square of a solid textured cotton or linen (front panel)

(8) 5" (12.7cm) squares of assorted prints (hexies)

22" (55.9cm) square of lightweight muslin (lining)

22" (55.9cm) square of coordinating fabric (pillow backing)

22" (55.9cm) square of batting

Other

20" (50.8cm) square pillow form

(8) 4" (10.2cm) hexagon cardstock templates (page 122)

16" (40.6cm) zipper in coordinating color

Basic quilting/sewing tools

Make the Pillow

1. Follow the directions on pages 24–25 to English paper-piece (8) 4" (10.2cm) hexies. Sew them together to form 2 side-by-side rows of 4.

2. Position the 2 rows on the front panel and pin in place. I placed mine left of center, but put yours anywhere you like. Keep in mind the final pillow casing will be 20" (50.8cm) square, so position away from outside seam allowances.

3. Appliqué the hexie rows onto the front panel using either a zigzag, straight stitch or decorative stitch; or you can hand appliqué them.

4. Sandwich the front panel, the batting and the muslin together, making sure to match raw edges. Baste together. Quilt as desired.

5. Trim the quilt sandwich to 20½" (52.1cm) square. Follow the instructions for installing a zipper on pages 26–27 to finish the pillow.

KALEIDOSCOPE QUILT
Risky Business

by Kelly

The little miracle of kaleidoscope blocks is that, when set together, they create a circular effect—without ever piecing a curve! This pattern is a true testament to creativity: Color placement is everything in this quilt, and by manipulating it, you can create an infinite number of designs.

FINISHED SIZE:	56½" × 80½"
	(143.5cm × 204.5cm)
LEVEL:	Intermediate

Materials

3½ yards (3.2m) of Fabric 1 (blue dot in sample)

1¾ yards (1.6m) of Fabric 2 (white/gray diamond in sample)

5 yards (4.6m) of fabric (backing)

⅝ yard (.6m) coordinating fabric (binding)

Batting

Thread

Other

The Kaleido-Ruler by Marti Michell (see Resources on page 125)

Basic quilting/sewing tools

Quilter's spray starch (optional; see Resources on page 125)

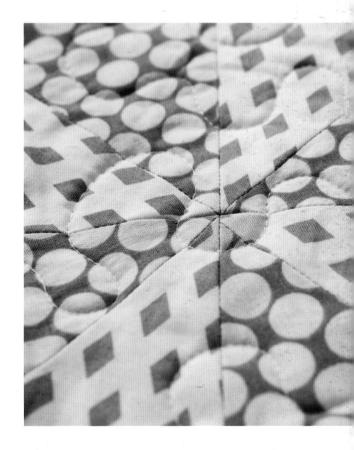

Make the Kaleidoscope Blocks

1. Cut (8) 6½" × WOF (16.5cm × WOF) strips each from Fabric 1 and Fabric 2. Press and spray starch the strips well.

2. Place the Kaleido-Ruler on top of one 6½" (16.5cm) wide strip, aligning the top blunt edge of the ruler with the top long edge of the strip, and the 12" (30.5cm) marking on the ruler with the bottom long edge of the strip. Carefully cut along both sides of the ruler to make your first wedge.

3. Turn the ruler 180 degrees, and align the blunt tip of the ruler with the bottom edge of the fabric, and the 12" (30.5cm) marking with the top edge of the fabric. Cut along the right-hand side of the ruler to make your second wedge (Figure 1).

4. Continue to flip the ruler and cut until you have cut as many wedges as you can from the strip. Cut all 16 of the 6½" (16.5cm) Fabric 1 and Fabric 2 strips in this way. You will need 96 Fabric 1 wedges and 96 Fabric 2 wedges.

5. Place a Fabric 1 wedge on top of a Fabric 2 wedge, right sides together (Figure 2). Starting at the outer point, sew them together along one long side (Figure 3). Press the seams open.

Note: Be careful that you sew the wedges together the same way each time, so that when you open them, Fabric 1 is always on the same side of Fabric 2.

6. In the same way, sew 2 of the wedge sections together to create a 4-wedge section (Figure 4). Press the seam open. Repeat to make (48) 4-wedge sections.

7. Place 2 of these 4-wedge sections right sides together, aligning them along the long straight edge. Pin them carefully, aligning the intersecting seams in the middle of the block. Sew along the edge to make an octagon (Figure 5). Press the seam open. Repeat to make 24 octagons.

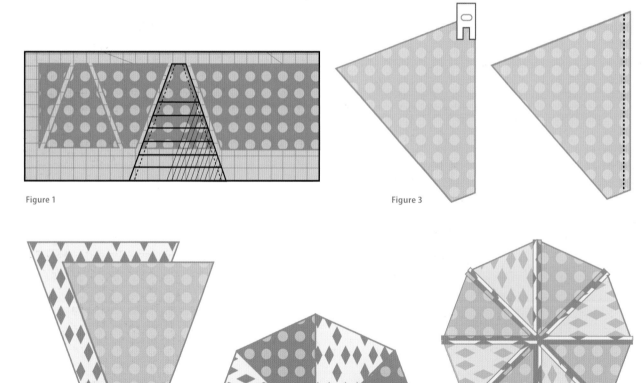

Figure 1

Figure 3

Figure 2

Figure 4

Figure 5

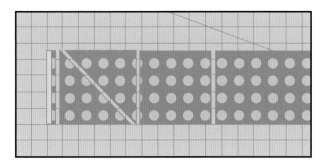

Figure 6

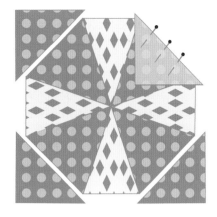

Figure 7

Figure 8

Figure 9

8. Press each of the octagons well, using spray starch if desired. Press firmly from the center out toward all the sides and corners.

9. Cut (6) 4⅞" (12.4cm) WOF strips from Fabric 1. Subcut the strips into (48) 4⅞" (12.4cm) squares. Cut each square once on the diagonal to make 96 triangles (Figure 6).

10. Place an octagon with Fabric 2 forming a cross (vertically and horizontally) and Fabric 1 in the corners. Pin and sew a Fabric 1 triangle to all 4 Fabric 1 corners of the octagon to form a square (Figure 7). Press. This is Block A (Figure 8). Make 12 A blocks.

11. Place an octagon with Fabric 1 forming a cross (vertically and horizontally) and Fabric 2 in the corners. Pin and sew a Fabric 1 triangle to all 4 Fabric 2 corners of the octagon to form a square. Press. This is Block B (Figure 9). Make 12 B blocks.

12. Trim each A and B block to 12½" (31.8cm) square.

13. Referring to the Layout Diagram on page 98, alternate A and B blocks in 6 rows of 4 blocks each. Sew the blocks into rows, and sew the rows together, carefully aligning and pinning all intersecting seams before sewing.

Make the Mini Kaleidoscope Blocks

1. Cut (1) 2½" × WOF (6.4cm × WOF) strip each of Fabric 1 and Fabric 2. Press and spray starch the strips well.

2. Using the Kaleido-Ruler, subcut 16 wedges from each strip. These wedges will be much smaller than before, but it's the same process.

Note: These wedges are so small, there is not a line marked on the ruler. To keep the wedges even, place the fabric strip along a horizontal line on your cutting mat. Place the blunt ruler tip even with the top edge of the fabric strip. Then make sure the horizontal lines of the ruler are parallel with a horizontal line on the cutting mat. Cut along the ruler side edges, flip the ruler, and continue cutting as before. Each time you flip the ruler, make sure a line on the ruler is aligned with a line on the cutting mat.

3. Cut (1) 3¼" × WOF (8.3cm × WOF) strip of Fabric 1. Subcut the strip into 3¼" (8.3cm) squares. Cut each square once on the diagonal to make 16 triangles.

4. In the same way that you pieced, pressed and trimmed the big blocks, make 2 mini A blocks and 2 mini B blocks.

Make the Borders and Finish the Quilt
Refer to the Layout Diagram as you complete the following steps.

1. Cut (7) 4½" × WOF (11.4cm × WOF) strips from Fabric 1.

2. From these strips, piece (2) 48½" (123.2cm) long strips. Sew one to the top edge and one to the bottom edge of the quilt. Press.

3. From the remaining 4½" (11.4cm) strips, piece (2) 72½" (184.2cm) strips. Sew 1 mini Block A to one end of each strip, and sew 1 mini Block B to the other end of each strip. Press.

4. Sew 1 of these strips to each side of the quilt so that mini Block A is at the top of the quilt on one side and at the bottom of the quilt on the other side. Press. This completes the quilt top.

5. Layer the quilt top with backing and batting, then baste and quilt. I used a wide meander over the entire quilt in a thread that blended. If you use wild prints like I did, the quilting gets lost, so functional quilting is all that is necessary.

6. Finish by binding with 2¼" (5.7cm) wide coordinating fabric strips.

Kelly says...
I love using wild and crazy prints together, and these two just spoke to me. Putting these fabrics together breaks all the "rules": not enough contrast, similar scale, too busy. But you know what? I love it, and that's all that matters! Do whatever floats your boat, listen to your gut and just go for it! You'll love a quilt that you took some risks on more than one that follows someone else's rules.

Layout Diagram

RISKY BUSINESS QUILT

Must Stash

by Kelly

I constantly find myself staring at a piece of my stash fabric, rotary cutter in hand and… I just can't cut it. Some pieces of fabric are flat-out too cool or special to chop up into little bits, or to make into a quilt to give away. Fussy-cut diamonds from your stash for this quilt so you'll always have a little piece of your favorites.

FINISHED SIZE:	44" × 58"
	(111.5cm × 147.3cm)
LEVEL:	Intermediate

Materials

72 large scraps, at least 6" × 10" (15.2cm × 25.4cm) (diamonds)

2¾ yards (2.5m) of gray background fabric (sashing, setting triangles, binding)

2½ yards (2.3m) (backing)

Batting

Thread

Other

5¼" × 9" (4.8cm × 22.9cm) diamond template (page 123; or see sidebar on page 102 to make)

Sheet of drawing/graph paper

Template plastic

Marking chalk

Basic quilting/sewing tools

Kelly says…

Consider starting a box or drawer in your sewing room specifically for this quilt. Every time you buy a new fabric you really love, cut a diamond and throw it in the box. Soon, you'll have a precut quilt featuring your favorite fabrics all ready to go together.

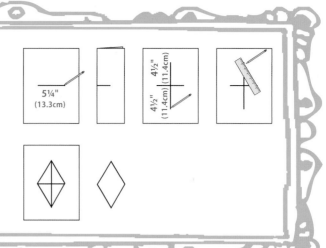

Kelly says…

To create the diamond template, on a sheet of drawing/graph paper, measure and draw a 5¼" (4.8cm) horizontal line. Fold the paper in half, matching the ends of the line to find the perpendicular center of the line. Through the center point, draw a perpendicular vertical line that measures 9" (22.9cm) in length, 4½" (11.4cm) on each side of the horizontal line. Connect the outside points to create a diamond. Cut and trace the paper diamond onto template plastic, cut it out and voilá—a template you can hang onto forever.

Make and Sash the Diamonds

1. From each of the 72 large fabric scraps, cut one diamond shape using the diamond template. Fussy-cut motifs and sections from the fabric as desired, centering the image in the diamond (Figure 1). From the gray background fabric, cut 26 gray diamonds of the same size.

2. Lay out the diamonds in diagonal rows as shown in Figure 2. I arranged mine in "rainbow order," but you can arrange yours however you like. A gray diamond should start and finish every diagonal row in the quilt and be placed in all four corners (Figure 2).

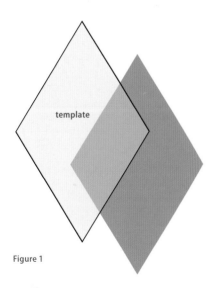

Figure 1

Figure 2

102

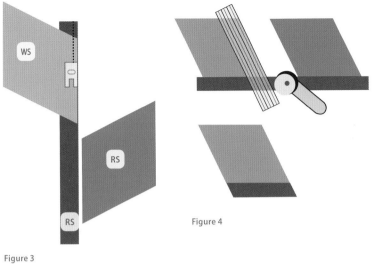

Figure 4

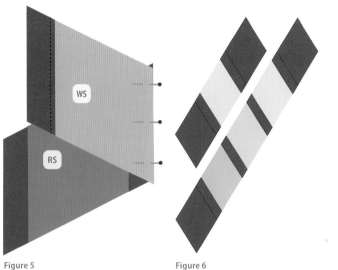

Figure 3

Figure 5

Figure 6

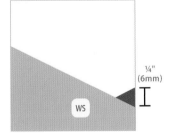

Figure 7

¼"
(6mm)

Figure 8

3. From the gray background fabric, cut (15) 1½" × WOF (3.8cm × WOF) sashing strips. With right sides together, chain sew the bottom left edge of each colorful stash diamond to the sashing strips (Figure 3). Sew sashing to the bottom left edge of each gray diamond that falls along the top side and right side of the quilt as well. (There's no need to sash the bottom and left-side gray diamonds.)

4. Press the sashing away from the diamond. Trim the sashing so it continues the lines of the adjacent edges of the diamond (Figure 4).

5. Sew the sashed diamonds together in diagonal rows (Figures 5 and 6). You will need to offset the pieces by ¼" (6mm) before sewing them together so that when the seam is opened, the edges align (Figure 7). Sew one first to get the hang of the alignment before chain-piecing all of them.

6. From the gray background fabric, cut (17) 11½" × WOF (29.2cm × WOF) sashing strips. Sew sashing strips along the right edge of each diagonal row of the quilt, leaving an extra 6" (15.2cm) "tail" of sashing fabric hanging off the top and bottom of each row. Piece the sashing strips together as necessary to sash the middle rows. Don't forget to sash the right-hand side of the top-left gray setting diamond (Figure 8).

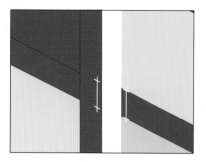

Figure 9

Finish the Quilt

1. Use the technique for matching diagonal seams on page 20 to carefully align the sashing across the diagonal rows (Figure 9). Pin and sew the diagonal rows together (Figure 10).

2. Trim the edges of the quilt into a rectangle by carefully cutting exactly where the setting triangles meet the edge of the sashing (Figures 11 and 12). This completes the quilt top.

3. Layer the quilt top with backing and batting. Baste and quilt. I used a dense quilting stitch in the sashing and a light, wavy echo stitch on the interior of each diamond. This makes the negative space of the sashing pop a bit, but doesn't detract from the fabric in the diamonds.

4. Finish by binding with 2¼" (xcm) wide gray background fabric strips.

Figure 10

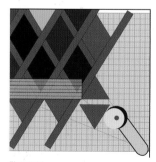

Figure 11

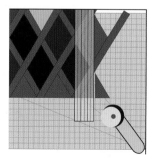

Figure 12

MUST STASH
QUILT

Midtown Girl

by Andie

This was an ambitious project from the beginning, to say the least. The degree of difficulty of this quilt, combined with the super-simple yet elegant black-and-white combo, made my tummy tickle a little. Not to mention, I had never made a pattern template from scratch. But, boy, do I love it.

Refer back to the Techniques section to learn how to paper-piece and sew a curved seam. Practice, practice, practice these skills before you dive into this project. Oh, and make one or two trial blocks before you cut into your fabric.

FINISHED SIZE:	49" × 49"
	(124.5cm × 124.5cm)
LEVEL:	Advanced
QUILTED BY:	Jenny Pedigo

Andie says…
When cutting out the pieces using Templates A and B, pay attention to the printed fabric's direction.

Materials

2 yards (1.8m) of predominantly black fabric with white graphic print (blocks, binding)

1 yard (.9m) of predominantly white fabric with black graphic print (blocks, cornerstones, binding)

3⅛ (2.9m) yards of white solid fabric (background)

3 yards (2.7m) of standard-width fabric or 1½ yards (1.4m) of 90" (228.6cm) wide fabric (backing)

Batting

Thread

Other

Basic quilting/sewing tools

Plastic template sheets

Chalk marking pencil

Templates A, B and C (page 124)

Paper-pieced curve/point pattern (page 124)

Cutting

From the black graphic print, cut:

- (180) 2½" × 3" (6.4cm × 7.6cm) rectangles
- 36 small inner curves using Template A

From the white graphic print fabric, cut:

- 36 middle curves using Template B
- (4) 2½" (6.4cm) squares for the cornerstones

From the white background fabric, cut:

- (144) 2½" × 3" (6.4cm × 7.6cm) rectangles
- (72) background pieces (36, plus 36 reversed) using Template C
- (12) 15" × 2½" (38.1cm × 6.4cm) strips for the sashing

Make the Block

1. Begin by tracing the templates on page 124 onto the template plastic, making sure to label them. Cut them out as explained in the "Cutting" section.

2. Make 36 copies of the paper-pieced curve with the points (page 124).

3. Referring to the paper-piecing technique on pages 22–23, paper-piece all 36 curve/point pieces. Use the small black print rectangles in the background area (points facing inward), and the small white solid rectangles in the points facing outward. Trim the finished curved units along the pattern's outer borders (Figure 1). Remove the paper backing.

4. Sew a white background piece and a reverse one cut from Template C together, making sure to sew along the correct side of the pieces (Figure 2). Press the seams open.

5. Referring to the "Sewing Curved Seams" section on page 21 and Figure 3, assemble the blocks:
- Sew the inner corner pieces (Template A pieces) to the middle curved pieces (Template B).
- Sew one of these units to each of the paper-pieced curves.
- Sew one of these units to each of the white background sections.

6. Press all seams toward the white background fabric.

7. Trim all 36 blocks to 7¾" × 7¾" (19.7cm × 19.7cm).

8. Now, assemble the large blocks, referring to Figure 4:
- Sew two small blocks together, sewing together the white background sides so that the curves are toward the center. Repeat this process, making 18 sets of pairs. Press seams open.
- Sew two of these pairs together so that all of the center and diagonal seams from the white background pieces match up in the middle. Press seams open. Repeat with all 18 sets of pairs to make 9 large blocks.

9. Trim each large block to 15¼" × 15¼" (38.7cm × 38.7cm).

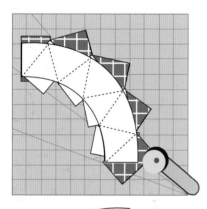

Figure 3

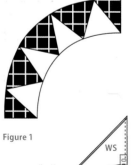

Figure 1

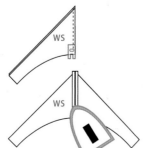

Figure 2

Figure 4

Assemble and Finish the Quilt

1. To make the two sashing strips, sew (3) 15" × 2½" (38.1cm × 6.4cm) white strips alternating with two cornerstones. Repeat to make a second sashing strip (Figure 5).

2. Referring to the Layout Diagram, lay out the 9 blocks in 3 rows of 3 blocks. Sew the remaining 6 sashing strips to the bottom of each block in the top 2 rows. Then sew the 3 vertical columns together.

3. Sew a vertical sashing strip to the right side of the left and center columns. Then sew the 3 columns together.

4. Layer the quilt top with backing and batting, then baste and quilt. See the sidebar on page 110 for more info on the quilting design for this quilt.

5. Finish by binding with 2¼" (5.7cm) wide white fabric strips.

Figure 5

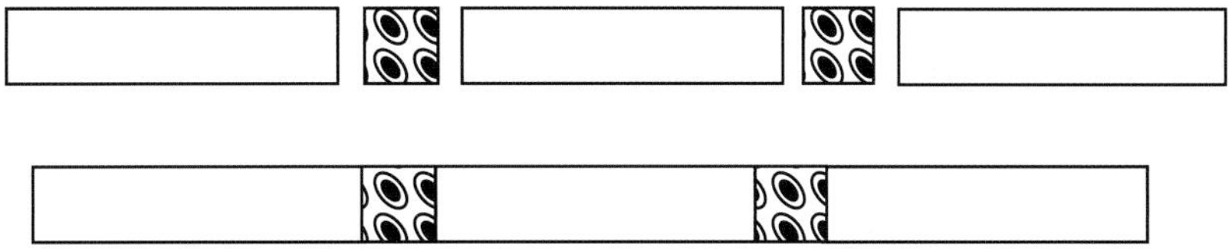

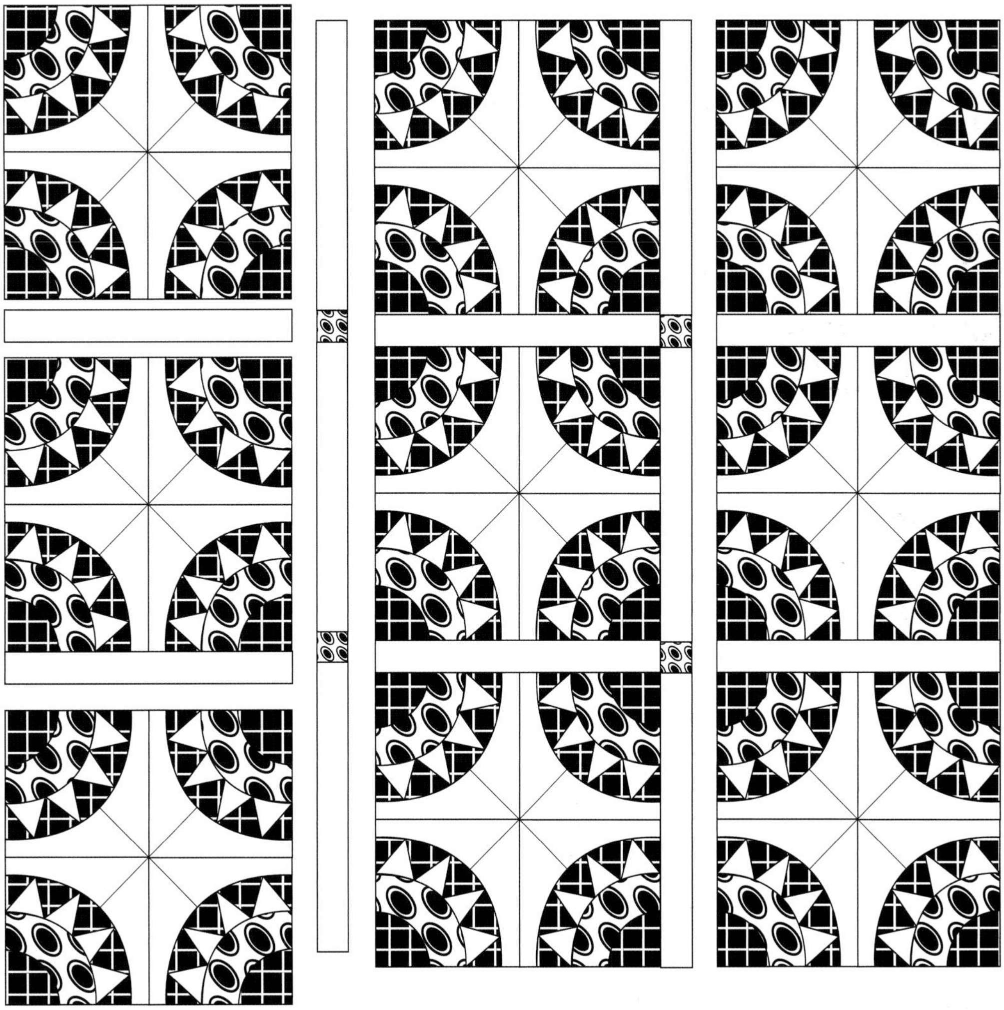

Layout Diagram

109

MIDTOWN GIRL QUILT

The Dresden Files

by Kelly

The Dresden plate always intimidated but intrigued me. I assumed making a successful block would be incredibly complicated, but it's not nearly as hard as you might think. With the exception of the center appliqués, there's not any curved sewing. This quilt is the perfect excuse to buy a little bit of an entire line of fabric; supplement here and there with your stash, and you've got a quilt with a ton of visual interest. The background lets the colors really pop and provides an area for adding extra interest with some fabulous quilting.

FINISHED SIZE:	86½" × 100½"
	(219.7cm × 255.3cm)
LEVEL:	Advanced
QUILTED BY:	Angela Walters

Materials

½ yard (.5m) each of 20 bright fabrics (Dresden plates, sashing, binding)

6 yards (5.5m) of background fabric

3 yards (2.7m) of 90" (228.6cm) wide fabric or 7½ yards (6.9m) of 40" (xcm) wide fabric (backing)

8" × 40" (20.3cm × 101.6cm) double-sided, lightweight fusible web

Batting

Thread for piecing and appliqué

Other

Circle template (page 122)

Easy Dresden Ruler by Darlene Zimmerman (see Resources on page 125)

Turning tool (for poking out corners)

Cardboard or template plastic

Pencil

Paper scissors

Basic quilting/sewing tools

Temporary basting spray

Quilter's spray starch (optional; see Resources on page 125)

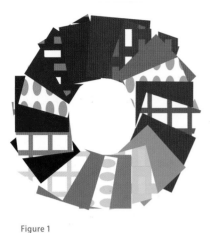

Figure 1

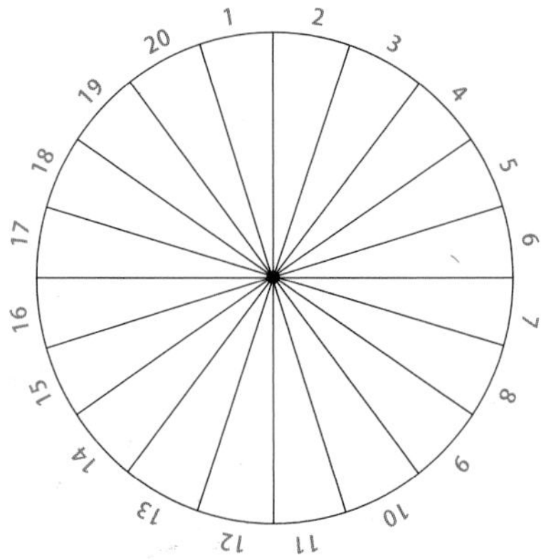

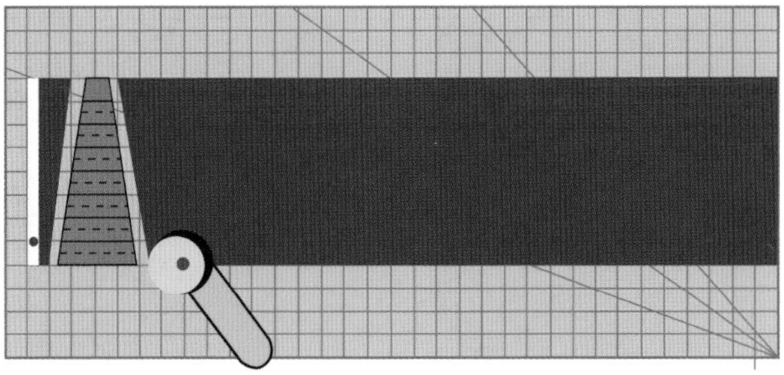

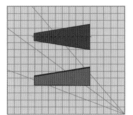

Figure 3

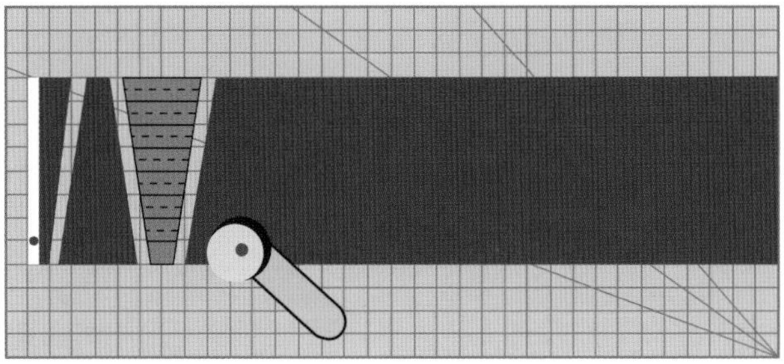

Figure 4

Figure 5

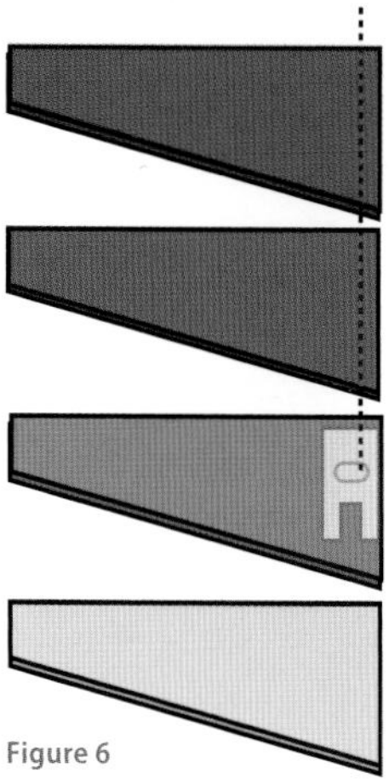

Figure 6

Figure 2

Make the Dresden Plates

1. Lay out your 20 bright fabrics in a circle, rearranging them until you are happy with the placement. Take a photo of the arrangement so you can remember it later, or draw and label a chart to help you remember (Figures 1 and 2).

2. From each of the bright fabrics, cut an 8" × WOF (20.3cm × WOF) strip.

3. Place the Easy Dresden Ruler on top of an 8" (20.3cm) wide strip, aligning the top straight edge of the ruler with the top long edge of the strip, and the bottom straight edge of the ruler with the bottom long edge of the strip. Carefully cut along both sides of the ruler to make your first wedge (Figure 3).

4. Turn the ruler 180 degrees, and again align the top and bottom edges of the ruler with the strip, and the side of the ruler with the cut edge of the strip. Cut along the other side of the ruler to make your second wedge (Figure 4). Continue cutting the strip into wedges to cut a total of 8 wedges.

5. Repeat steps 3 and 4 to cut 8 wedges from each of the 20 bright fabrics.

6. Fold each wedge in half lengthwise, right sides together, carefully aligning the edges (Figure 5).

7. Starting at the fold and using a ¼" (6mm) seam, sew along the long top edge of each folded wedge (Figure 6).

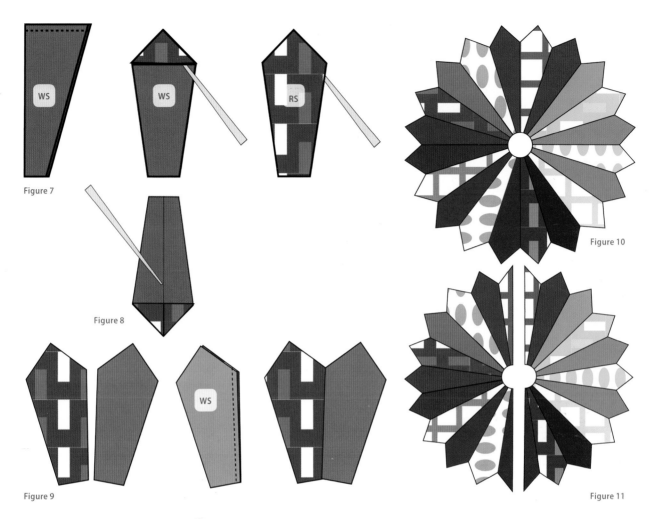

Figure 7

Figure 8

Figure 9

Figure 10

Figure 11

8. Turn each wedge right side out, using a turning tool to gently poke out the tips (Figure 7).

9. Press the tip and sides of each wedge flat, aligning the seam line in the tip with the fold line through the center of the wedge (Figure 8).

10. Using the fabric arrangement guide you made in step 1, arrange all of the wedges into 8 circles, each with 20 different fabrics.

11. Using a ¼" (6mm) seam, sew 2 adjacent wedges together, being sure to maintain the fabric order as you sew (Figure 9). Press seams to the side.

12. Continue until you have sewn 20 adjacent wedges together into a Dresden plate (Figure 10). Repeat to sew 8 plates.

Note: It is more important that your wedges align with each other properly on the outside of the plate rather than at the center, since the area where the fabric comes together at the center of the plate will be covered later with a circle appliqué. When you sew your wedges together, make sure they are aligned at the outside tips, and sew from the outside to the center to maintain this alignment.

13. Press the plates well, using spray starch if necessary.

14. Cut 2 of the finished Dresden plates perfectly in half (Figure 11).

Figure 12

Figure 13

Make the Background and Appliqué the Plates

1. From the background fabric, cut (20) 20½" (52.1cm) squares.

2. From the bright plate fabrics, cut (5)2½" × 20½" (6.4cm × 52.1cm) red sashing strips, (5) 2½" × 20½" (6.4cm × 52.1cm) purple sashing strips, and (5) 2½" × 20½" (6.4cm × 52.1cm) blue/green sashing strips.

3. Sew the sashing strips to the background squares as shown in Figure 12. Press seams to the side. Do not sew the entire background together at this point—only sew the 6 small sections indicated.

4. Place 4 full and 2 half Dresden plates on the background sections (Figure 13). Use the seam lines to help you align the plates perfectly in the center of the blocks, and use temporary basting spray and pins to hold the plates in place.

5. Use a short stitch length and a neutral/matching thread to stitch around the outside edge of each plate to sew it to the background section (Figure 14).

6. Sew the background sections together to form the complete quilt background. Press seams to the side.

7. In the same way as before, sew the remaining 2 full and 1 half Dresden plates to the center of the quilt background, referring to the full quilt image for placement.

8. Cut a circle from cardboard or template plastic that is approximately 4" (10.2cm) in diameter (or use the circle template).

9. From the background fabric, cut (8) 5" (12.7cm) squares. Following the manufacturer's instructions, iron double-sided lightweight fusible web to the wrong side of each square. Trace around the circle template onto the paper side of the fusible web.

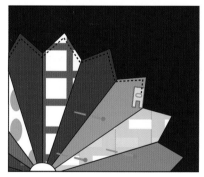

Figure 14

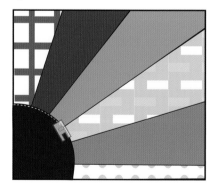

Figure 15

10. Cut out each circle. Cut two of the circles in half. Remove the paper backing from the fusible web.

11. Fuse each circle or half-circle to the center of each Dresden plate. Make sure the circle covers all of the plate's raw edges.

12. Using matching thread and a short stitch length, stitch around the outside of each center circle very close to the edge (Figure 15). This completes the quilt top.

Finish the Quilt

1. Layer the quilt top with backing and batting, then baste and quilt. Unlike some of the other quilts in the book, this quilt really lends itself to some intricate quilting—it can take it! Angela quilted a lattice through the entire background, and then filled in the lattice section with a variety of swirls.

2. Finish by binding with 2¼" (5.7cm) wide bright fabric strips.

Note: I cut my 2¼" (5.7cm) binding strips at different lengths before sewing them together in order to create a scrappy binding effect. You will need approximately 385" (9.8m) of binding for this quilt.

Kelly says...
I highly recommend sewing a test Dresden plate with scrap fabrics first. If your plates don't lie flat once they are sewn together, try reducing your seam allowance just a smidge. This will help ease out any extra fullness.

THE DRESDEN FILES QUILT (BACK)
I pieced the backing for this quilt using leftover scraps from the Dresden plate fabrics. I like the fact that my quilt is interesting on the back as well as the front, and now I don't have a bunch of scraps hanging around my sewing room that I'll probably never use.

THE DRESDEN FILES QUILT

Offset Dresden Pillow

by Kelly

I love a sensible quilted pillow, and this one's perfect to try your hand at making a Dresden plate before diving into a huge quilt project. This is a great method for turning any orphan blocks lying around into comfy throw pillows.

FINISHED PILLOW SIZE:
15" square (38.1cm)

LEVEL: Intermediate

Materials

20 coordinating charm squares (Dresden plate)

16" × 16" (40.6cm × 40.6cm) square and 5" × 5" (12.7cm × 12.7cm) square of background fabric

½ yard (.5m) of contrasting fabric (backing)

5" × 5" (12.7cm × 12.7cm) double-sided lightweight fusible web

Batting

Neutral/coordinating thread (appliqué)

Contrasting thread (quilting/satin stitch)

15" (38.1cm) pillow form

Other

Circle template (page 122)

Easy Dresden Ruler by Darlene Zimmerman (see Resources on page 125)

Turning tool (for poking out corners)

Basic quilting/sewing tools

Quilter's spray starch (optional; see Resources on page 125)

Make the Pillow

1. From each of the 20 charm squares, cut a 5" (12.7cm) tall wedge using the Easy Dresden Ruler.

Note: If you are careful, you can cut two wedges from each charm square. Set the second wedge aside to make a second Dresden plate for another project (or a second pillow).

2. Fold each wedge in half lengthwise, right sides together, carefully aligning the edges.

3. Starting at the fold and using a ¼" (6mm) seam, sew along the long top edge of each folded wedge.

4. Turn each wedge right side out, using a turning tool to gently poke out the tips.

5. Press the tip and sides of each wedge flat, aligning the seam line in the tips with the fold lines through the centers of the wedges.

6. Arrange and sew all 20 wedges into a circle. Press seams to the side.

7. Press the plate well, using spray starch if necessary. Position it as desired on the 16" (40.6cm) square of background fabric.

Note: I offset my plate but you can center it if you like. However you position the plate, be sure to keep it at least 1" (2.5cm) away from the edges of the background square.

8. Use a short stitch length and a neutral/matching thread to stitch around the outside edge of the plate to secure it to the background square.

9. Following the manufacturer's instructions, iron double-sided lightweight fusible web to the wrong side of the 5" (12.7cm) background square. Draw and cut out a circle at least 4" (10.2cm) in diameter (or use the template). Remove the paper backing from the fusible web. Fuse the circle to the center of the Dresden plate. Make sure the circle covers all of the plate's raw edges.

10. Place the pillow cover right side up on top of a piece of batting that is slightly bigger than the cover. Use a contrasting thread to quilt the entire pillow top (Figure 1). Then use the same thread to satin stitch around the edge of the center circle.

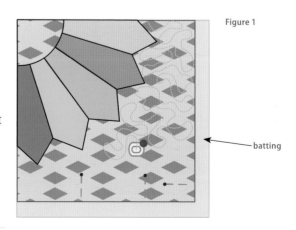

Figure 1

batting

11. Trim the edges of the batting even with the edges of the pillow cover.

12. From the backing fabric, cut (2) 11" × 16" (27.9cm × 40.6cm) rectangles. On each rectangle, fold one long edge under by ¼" (6mm). Press the fold in place. Then fold under a second time to conceal the raw edge (Figure 2).

13. Topstitch the folded edge in place on both rectangles (Figure 3).

14. Lay the pillow top face up on a worktable. Place a backing rectangle right side down on top of the pillow top, aligning the raw edges and placing the folded edge toward the center of the pillow (Figure 4).

15. Layer the second backing piece onto the pillow in the same way, so the entire pillow top is covered and the folded edges of the backing sections are overlapping the middle of the pillow (Figure 5).

16. Carefully pin the backing pieces to the pillow top, pinning around the perimeter of the pillow.

17. Using a ½" (1.3cm) seam allowance, sew around the entire perimeter of the pillow, backstitching where the backing pieces overlap and at the corners.

18. Trim off the corners, cutting outside of the stitching lines (Figure 6).

19. Turn the pillowcase through the center hole and insert a 15" (38.1cm) pillow form to finish.

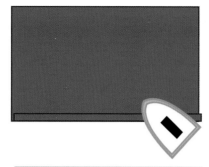

Figure 2

Figure 3

Figure 4

Figure 5

Figure 6

Templates and Patterns

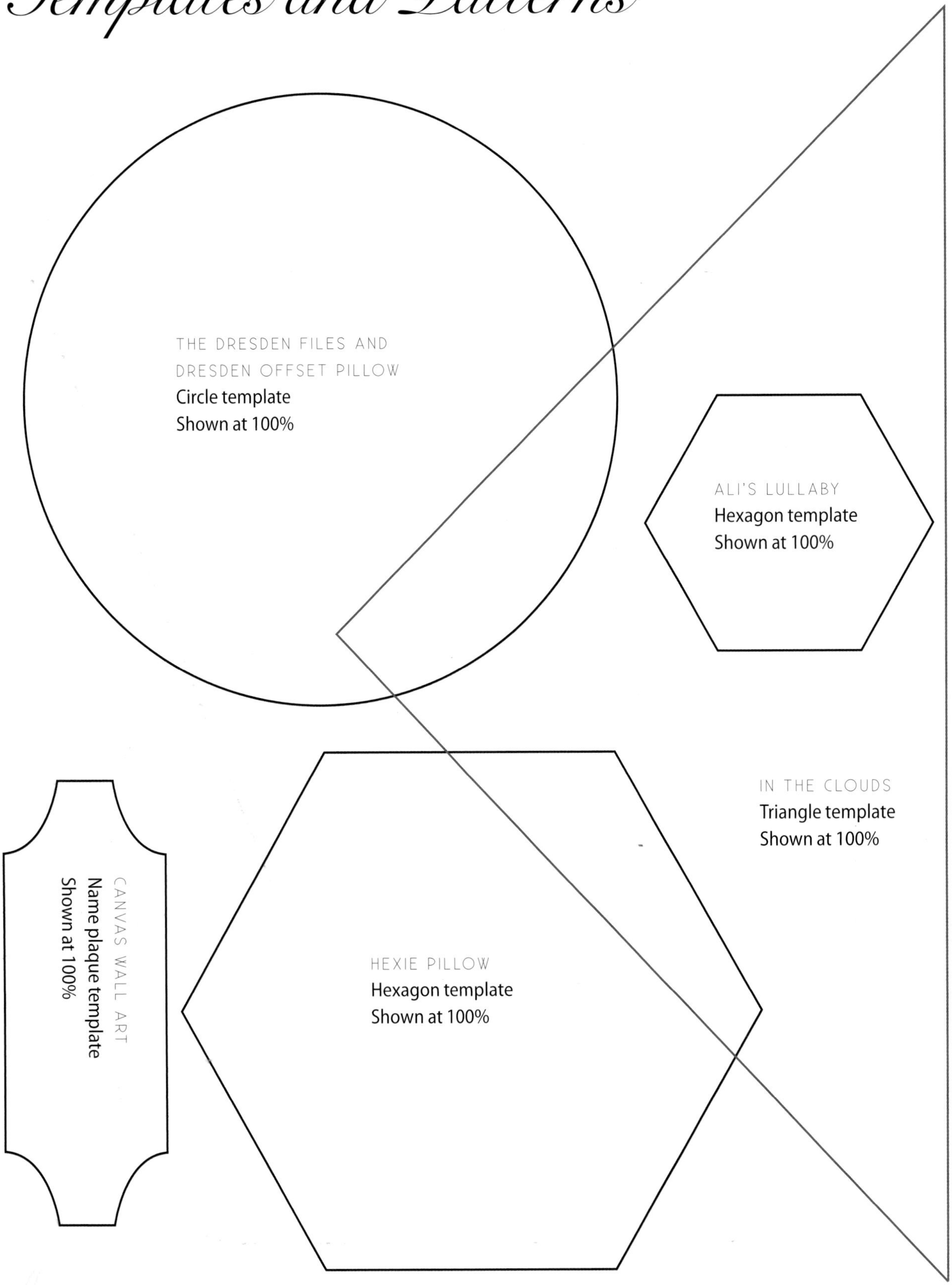

THE DRESDEN FILES AND
DRESDEN OFFSET PILLOW
Circle template
Shown at 100%

ALI'S LULLABY
Hexagon template
Shown at 100%

IN THE CLOUDS
Triangle template
Shown at 100%

CANVAS WALL ART
Name plaque template
Shown at 100%

HEXIE PILLOW
Hexagon template
Shown at 100%

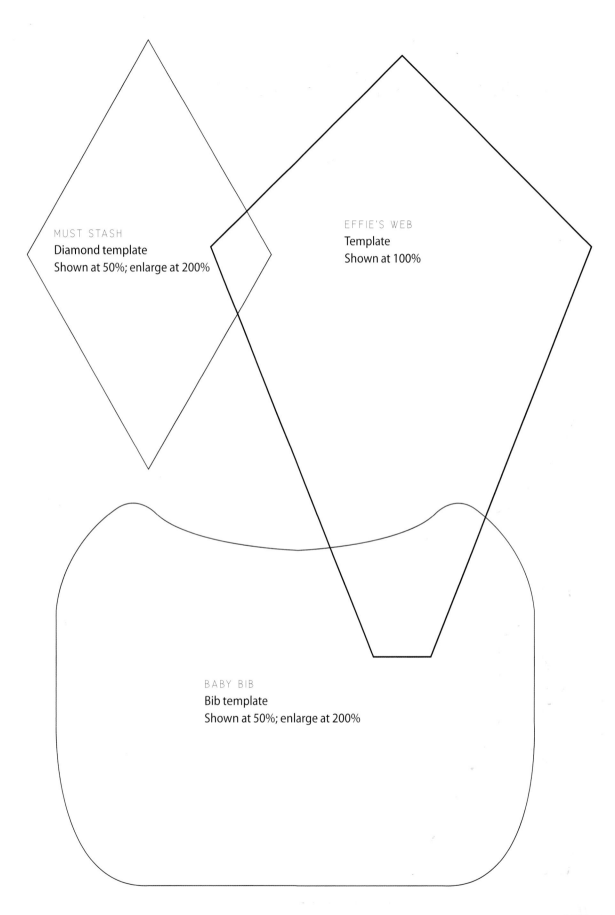

MUST STASH
Diamond template
Shown at 50%; enlarge at 200%

EFFIE'S WEB
Template
Shown at 100%

BABY BIB
Bib template
Shown at 50%; enlarge at 200%

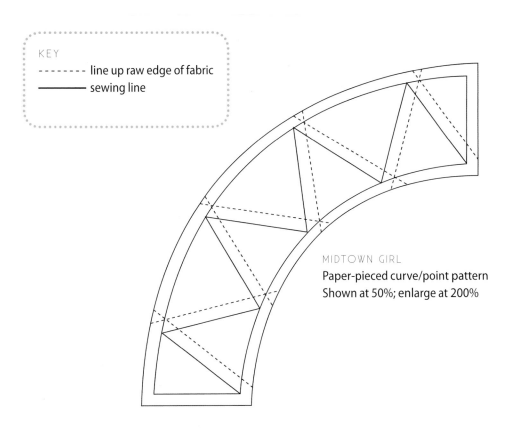

MIDTOWN GIRL
Paper-pieced curve/point pattern
Shown at 50%; enlarge at 200%

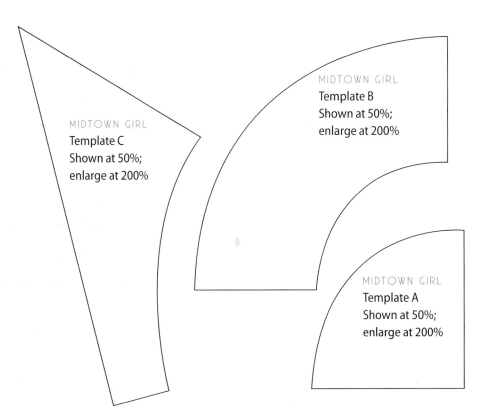

MIDTOWN GIRL
Template C
Shown at 50%;
enlarge at 200%

MIDTOWN GIRL
Template B
Shown at 50%;
enlarge at 200%

MIDTOWN GIRL
Template A
Shown at 50%;
enlarge at 200%

Index

Resources

Alexander Henry Fabrics
www.ahfabrics.com
The Ghastlies fabric

Best Press spray starch
maryellenproducts.com

**Easy Dresden Ruler by
Darlene Zimmerman**
www.feedsacklady.com/tools.php

Kaleido-Ruler by Marti Michell
www.frommarti.com

The Modern Quilt Guild
themodernquiltguild.com

Robert Kaufman Fabrics
www.robertkaufman.com
Dusty Kona Rollup fabric

About the Authors

KELLY BISCOPINK is an editor, blogger, sister, daughter, best friend, sewist, quilter, fabric hoarder, pattern maker, seam ripper, reader, writer, list creator, travel enthusiast, theater lover, tap dancer, piano player and cupcake baker from Cincinnati, Ohio. Kelly loves all things quilted and stitchy, and enjoys sharing her creative process on her blog, Stitchy Quilt Stuff (StitchyQuiltStuff.blogspot.com).

ANDREA JOHNSON is wife to her college sweetheart and mama to three teenagers. She's been sewing since age 14, after learning to sew in a high school Home Ec class. She loves to sew and quilt, and truly enjoys the construction process of making something beautiful and functional. When she's not sewing, she is cooking, baking, gardening, volunteering, boating, traveling, watching hockey and reading. She blogs at AndieJohnsonSews.blogspot.com and teaches at quilt shops and quilting events all over. Drop Andie a line and say hello anytime at andiejohnsonsews@gmail.com.

Kelly's Acknowledgments

A huge THANK YOU goes out…

To my family, friends, acquaintances, neighbors, friends-of-friends, coworkers and everyone I let see my Facebook page: Thank you for the help, support and encouragement, not just while writing this book, but for all of the times I've been a bit of a psychopath while working on a project. I thank you in advance for your continued support as I build my empire and take over the world, one sewing machine at a time.

To my editors, Kristy Conlin and Stef Laufersweiler—thank you for your guidance, organization and for spellchequing my book; and thank you to Kaysie Schreiner and Sarah Clark for making it beautiful. Thanks to everyone at F+W who helped to make this book a reality.

To my dad, Jerry, for being, well, pretty much the best dad ever—a title awarded for a myriad of reasons including, but not limited to, cleaning and oiling my sewing machine.

To my sister, Karen, for just "getting" me. You are now and will always be my bestie. TMAIB.

To my mom, Alice, for so many things, but most importantly in the context of this book, for teaching me how to sew, and for introducing me to this world of quilting that I have fallen in love with and spent all of my money pursuing. (And also, for binding half of the quilts in the book…) This truly would never have happened without you.

And to my coauthor, Andie—I can't imagine tackling this project with anyone else. Dang, girl, we did it—let's open that champagne!

Andie's Acknowledgments

Thank you to my friends who have supported and tolerated me throughout this process; to our editors, Kristy Conlin and Stef Laufersweiler, and the entire staff of F+W Media, who made this book a reality; Mrs. Laura White, for teaching me how to sew; my parents, for giving me the gift of creativity; all of the quilting friends I've met online and in real life, who have inspired me and taught me oodles of stuff; and most importantly to God, for dropping this amazing quilty blessing square in my lap.

To my family: Thank you for believing in me, encouraging me, tolerating me and allowing me to follow a dream.

Kel Kel Lollybritches: I love you. Like, I really love you. So grateful that I was smart enough to hitch my wagon to your star!

For Chris, Katie, Sam and Chas

www.fwmedia.com

16 15 14 13 12   5 4 3 2 1

Distributed in Canada by Fraser Direct
100 Armstrong Avenue
Georgetown, ON, Canada L7G 5S4
Tel: (905) 877-4411

Distributed in the U.K. and Europe by F&W MEDIA INTERNATIONAL
Brunel House, Newton Abbot, Devon, TQ12 4PU, England
Tel: (+44) 1626 323200, Fax: (+44) 1626 323319
Email: enquiries@fwmedia.com

Distributed in Australia by Capricorn Link
P.O. Box 704, S. Windsor NSW, 2756 Australia
Tel: (02) 4577-3555

SRN: W7394

ISBN-13: 978-1-4402-2968-8
ISBN-10: 1-4402-2968-6

Edited by Kristin Conlin and Stefanie Laufersweiler
Designed by Sarah Clark
Production coordinated by Greg Nock
Photographed by Christine Polomsky, Lorna Yabsley, Jack Kirby and Ric Deliantoni
Illustrated by Kaysie Schreiner

METRIC CONVERSION CHART

To convert	to	multiply by
Inches	Centimeters	2.54
Centimeters	Inches	0.4
Feet	Centimeters	30.5
Centimeters	Feet	0.03
Yards	Meters	0.9
Meters	Yards	1.1

Measurements have been given in imperial inches with metric conversions in parentheses. Use one or the other as they are not interchangeable. The most accurate results will be obtained using inches.

Connect — Inspire — Create

Join our online craft community for exclusive offers and daily doses of inspiration.

 fwcraft   @fwcraft

SEW TO SWAP
Quilting Projects to Exchange Online & by Mail

by Chrissie Grace

Gather a group of quilting friends and start trading fabric, quilt blocks and full projects for the ultimate community sewing activity! From fabric to block to project exchanges, Chrissie Grace and her team of popular contributors show you the best way to organize and run your very own swap while making 12 beautiful projects.

QUILTS FROM THE HOUSE OF TULA PINK
20 Fabric Projects to Make, Use & Love

by Tula Pink

Welcome to the world of cutting-edge fabric designer, Tula Pink, where clever quilts show off fanciful fabric, and your imagination can be let out to play. Between 10 amazing quilts and 10 extra-cool companion projects, you'll be inspired to play with fabric, color and design in a way like never before!

PRE-CUT COMBO QUILTS
14 Quilts that Blend Jelly Rolls, Layer Cakes, Turnovers and More

by Debra Fehr Greenway

Discover exciting quilt possibilities by blending different types and sizes of pre-cut fabrics! With instructions for 14 quilts and 5 variations, you'll be inspired to start sewing with your favorite fabrics and pre-cut stash. Each pattern is also fat quarter friendly, featuring instructions for both fat quarters and pre-cuts.

 These and other fine Krause Publications titles are available at your local craft retailer, bookstore or online supplier, or visit our website at Store.MarthaPullen.com.